UNFINISHED PUZZLE

Cuban Agriculture:
The Challenges, Lessons
& Opportunities

"To produce food for the people is revolutionary," slogan of a Cuban agroecological farm

Food First Books
Institute for Food and Development Policy
398 60th Street, Oakland, CA 94618-1212 USA
Tel (510) 654-4400   Fax (510) 654-4551
www.foodfirst.org   foodfirst@foodfirst.org

Developmental editing by *Eric Holt-Giménez*
Translation from the Spanish language edition by *Tanya Kerssen*
Photos by *Mikel Marrota and May Ling Chan*
Cover and text design by *Martha Katigbak-Fernandez*

Library of Congress Cataloging-in-Publication Data

Chan, May Ling, 1962-
  Unfinished puzzle : Cuban agriculture: the challenges, lessons and opportunities /
[May Ling Chan and Eduardo Francisco Freyre Roach] ; translated by Tanya Kerssen.
    p. cm.
  Translated from Spanish.
  Translation of: Cuba atando cabos: la agricultura Cubana: contratiempos, reajustes
y desafios.
  Includes bibliographical references.
  ISBN 978-0-935028-40-9 ((e-book)) -- ISBN 978-0-935028-42-3 ((print version):
alk. paper)
  1. Agriculture--Cuba. 2. Agriculture and state--Cuba. I. Freyre Roach, Eduardo
Francisco, 1958- II. Institute for Food and Development Policy (Oakland, Calif.)
III. Title. IV. Title: Cuban agriculture : the challenges, lessons and opportunities.
V. Title: Cuba atando cabos.
  S177.C43 2012
  338.1097291--dc23

                              2012037862

Cuba Unfinished Puzzle: Cuban Agriculture: The Challenges, Lessons and
Opportunities / May Ling Chan and Eduardo Francisco Freyre Roach

Food First Books are distributed by
Perseus Distribution
250 West 57th Street
New York, NY 10107
Tel 212.340.8100
www.perseusdistribution.com

Printed in Canada.
5 4 3 2 1

ABOUT THE AUTHORS

May Ling Chan worked with Oxfam Hong Kong in Asia and Africa for over 12 years. She did research on agricultural policy, agroecology and incentive structures for sustainable production from 2005 to 2009 at the Agrarian University of Havana (UNAH) in Cuba. maylingvida@gmail.com.

Eduardo Francisco Freyre Roach, PhD, has been a professor at UNAH for 27 years, specializing in rural sociology, sustainable agriculture and bioethics. freyre.roach2007@gmail.com.

ACKNOWLEDGMENTS

This report was made possible thanks to the support of Oxfam International in Cuba. Translation of this report, from Spanish into English, was sponsored by the Partnerships for Community Development.

The authors wish to thank the following people for their contributions: Armando Nova González for consulting support; Raisa Pages, Reina Rosa Mesa Herrera, Yuddelys Puebla Ortiz, Braulio Machín Sosa, Ricardo Delgado, Guillermo Betancourt, Eduardo Cuesta, Clara Trujillo, and Peter Rosset for their invaluable comments; Nilda Pérez Consuegra and Ramón Montano for their collaborative research; and Mikel Marrota for his photographs.

For the Spanish edition of this publication the authors wish to acknowledge Alberto Chanona for editing; Eduardo Martínez for cover design and Chan Gee San Teresa for text design and report production.

For this English edition the authors thank Eric Holt-Giménez for his vision in transforming the report into a book; Tanya Kerssen for translation; Marilyn Borchardt, William Wroblewski and Julie Powell for review; and Martha Katigbak-Fernandez for copy editing, design and production.

The contents of this report do not necessarily reflect the opinion of Oxfam.

The information in this publication was correct at the time of going to press.

TABLE OF CONTENTS

EXECUTIVE SUMMARY

Cuba is widely recognized for its social achievements including health care, education, social security, subsidized food and other benefits and opportunities, despite well-meaning, or sometimes not so well-meaning, international criticisms. For more than 50 years, this Caribbean island has defended and sustained these economic, political, social and cultural gains, and has maintained a commitment to humanitarianism and international solidarity that persists to this day.

Throughout the world there is great interest in understanding the Cuban food system. Some basic questions that arise include:

How has this tiny Caribbean nation faced the challenges of climate change, neoliberal globalization and the global food crisis?

Why is the Cuban experience so unique in terms of sustainable agriculture, local development, agrarian reform, food security and food sovereignty?

Is the Cuban experience replicable in other countries, in both Latin America and the rest of the world?

This report addresses these questions using statistical data analysis, interviews and studies of the national and international context within which the Cuban food system has developed—including the many challenges and opportunities foreseen for the coming years.

We carried out field research in five out of Cuba's fourteen provinces (Pinar del Río, La Habana, Ciudad de La Habana, Sancti Spiritus and Guantánamo). During the course of this fieldwork, we conducted interviews with farmers, rural families, cooperatives, agricultural enterprises, government officials, members of nongovernmental organizations (NGOs), professionals and other relevant social actors.

Part one describes the socioeconomic context of Cuban agriculture, the natural environment that affect it and the international political context in which it has developed. This section concludes with an overview of the trends in production, consumption and agricultural imports and exports, focusing on 1989 to 2011.

Part two explores the unique agricultural policies Cubans implemented to confront the food and economic crises of the early 1990s.

Finally, part three examines the lessons to be learned from the Cuban experience with respect to local development, sustainable agriculture, agroecology, food security and food sovereignty. In particular, this section highlights the elements of the Cuban system most suitable for replication in other countries facing similar circumstances or challenges.

INTRODUCTION

Cuba is, without a doubt, a unique case: it is a multiethnic island state with a distinct political system that has evolved under a half-century-long economic blockade by the United States. These factors have influenced the country's historical development and will continue to define its future course.

This report contributes to the analysis of fundamental questions relating to Cuban agriculture, and of the challenges and setbacks it faces. First and foremost, we hope to deepen the understanding of the context in which the country's agricultural development unfolds.

Cuba navigates the turbulent waters of the dominant international economic and political order. Of course, "order" may be an overstatement, considering the proliferation of recent financial crises and oil- and food-price hikes that have affected rich and poor countries alike. In Cuba, the impact of these crises is magnified by the 50-year-US blockade. Nonetheless, by 2010 Cuba had begun opening its economic doors thanks to its integration into the Bolivarian Alliance for the Americas (ALBA), the Southern Common Market (MERCOSUR), Petrocaribe, the Caribbean Community (CARICOM) and the Rio Group.[1] The country currently practices bilateral trade with Venezuela, Vietnam, China, Brazil and other countries, including the United States.

Severe weather conditions have had a harsh impact on the island. Intense cyclones, accompanied by periods of prolonged drought, have ravaged the country. These natural disasters exacerbate soil erosion, thus making agricultural production increasingly difficult. Cuba has taken significant measures to minimize and mitigate these impacts.

---

[1] "Rio Group" refers to the Permanent Mechanism for Consultation and Coordination, established on December 18, 1986, within the framework of the Declaration of Río de Janeiro, signed by Argentina, Brazil, Colombia, Mexico, Panama, Peru, Uruguay and Venezuela. Cuba joined the bloc in November 2008.

In the last ten years, agricultural production has improved, but remains unstable and insufficient. Favorable results are seen with tubers, vegetables, fruit and small livestock. But persistent difficulties remain in the production of fresh milk, beef, chicken and, especially, sugarcane. Because domestic production has been insufficient to guarantee the island's food security, it has had to import food and suffer all of the consequences that this entails. To counter rising food prices in 2007, the government instituted a policy of import substitution, especially in the subsidized food basket, which includes beans, rice, corn, milk, eggs and chicken. This approach has been somewhat successful in diversifying production, consumption and agricultural exports.

The Cuban government continues to readjust its agricultural policies in strategic ways. In the late 1980s, the country fell into a deep crisis as a result of the collapse of the Soviet Bloc. To make matters worse, the United States intensified its blockade. These events provoked the immediate reduction of oil imports by 53%, food imports by 50% and fertilizers by 80% (Sinclair and Thompson 2001). As a result, the government declared a "Special Period in Peacetime of total austerity." The implementation of this extreme measure didn't mean that the government sat back and did nothing, however. The country was in urgent need of solutions. By the early 1990s, the government set in motion a series of transformations, both temporary and long term, in the agricultural sector. The goal, which remains to this day, was to overcome the problems caused by the input intensive, industrial trade agricultural model adopted in the 1960s. The changes implemented included:

- Granting vacant lands in usufruct to individuals, farmworker collectives or organizations willing and able to immediately make them productive in a sustainable manner
- Strengthening cooperatives
- Changing marketing regulations so that producers receive a higher price for their crops on the market, thus ensuring a greater availability and access to food
- Readjusting (with some difficulty) the size and importance of the sugarcane sector

The enormous challenges faced by Cuban agriculture are a source of intense debate on the island. On the one hand, since Cuba imports a large volume of food, some allege that the country is far from achieving food sovereignty. On the other hand, others argue that Cuba is in complete control of the decisions it makes about its food system. In fact, the government strongly supports Cuban farmers and promotes local self-sufficiency and sustainable agriculture as a matter of policy.

Organic production (regulated and certified) is booming in Cuba, especially when one looks at the production and export of organic citrus, coffee, honey and sugar. There is also strong debate about how to certify organic production and create differentiated markets for organic products without jeopardizing social equity.

Cuban research on genetically modified (GM) crops and animals has been highly controversial. In 2008 Cuban biotechnology researchers and genetic engineers produced a variety of transgenic maize resistant to the insect *palomilla* (*Spodoptera frugiperda*). The country began planting the GM maize on a small scale the following year, under regulatory oversight by the Biosafety Law, which regulates the planting and importation of genetically modified organisms (GMOs). But many argue that Cuba can and must remain GM free in order to protect the government-supported model of ecological agriculture and to protect the island's native seeds from contamination by GMOs.

In recent years Cuba has granted much greater support to locally managed development projects and sustainable agriculture. With the administrative decentralization promoted by the state, local actors have gained greater autonomy and decision-making power. As a result, a number of programs and development projects have been able to focus on:

- Building on local potential and local innovations
- Achieving a high degree of institutionalization and popularization
- Emphasizing community-based action, participation and management
- Creating networks among the various projects—although there continue to be challenges in this area
- Collaborating with the government and/or with NGOs

- Promoting low-external-input farming methods
- Facilitating dialogue and cooperation between traditional and scientific knowledge
- Establishing incentives, recognition and awards for farmers

These projects have indisputably made tremendous achievements in advancing sustainable agriculture in Cuba. For instance, researchers Peter Rosset and Martín Bourque (2001, xiii) note:

> In the midst of a global food crisis with ecological, economic and social repercussions, there are numerous examples throughout the world of farmer-led, community-based development that are economically viable. However, Cuba is one of the few examples where these projects have translated into policy changes and where substantial government resources have been invested in supporting this movement.

Similarly, World Bank expert Dale Allen Pfeiffer stated in 2005, "Cuba has disproved the myth that organic agriculture cannot maintain a modern nation." Richard Levins (2005) further added that, in Cuba, the ecologists have won the battle against the industrial model.

Cuban achievements in agriculture and sustainable development are recognized internationally. In 1996, the Cuban Movement for Organic Agriculture was awarded the Saar Mallinskrodt Prize by the International Federation of Organic Agriculture Movements (IFOAM). Three years later, in 1999, it was awarded the alternative Nobel Prize, the Right Livelihood Award. According to the World Wildlife Fund's Living Planet Report (2006), Cuba is the only country in the world that meets its criteria for "ecological footprint and sustainable development."[2] In 2010, the Goldman Prize, widely considered to be the "green" Nobel Prize, was awarded to the Program for Local Agricultural Innovation (PIAL) of the National Institute of Agricultural Science (INCA), for its contributions to biodiversity, agroecological innovation and local development.

---

[2] "Ecological footprint" is a concept related to the amount consumed by the average of citizen and the resources used to produce the goods and services consumed. This requires ensuring that resource extraction does not exceed the regenerative capacity of those resources.

Cuba continues to gain recognition for its ability to overcome the collapse of its food system in the 1990s and to maintain remarkable social achievements despite its isolation from international institutions including the IMF and the World Bank.

Cuba has rejected the neoliberal model, and fervently protects its political sovereignty. In 2001, World Bank president James Wolfensohn and head of the Data Management Group on Development, Eric Swanson, called Cuba an "anti-model" with the best health and education indicators in the developing world. And while the situation remains highly complex, Cuba's agricultural policies continue to satisfy the nutritional needs of its population, while ensuring a high degree of social equity that meets the needs of both producers and consumers. As such, the island meets a number of development criteria that are recognized the world over (Sinclair and Thompson 2001).

Moving forward, it is useful to take into account not only the successes, but also the difficulties that have emerged along the way. Cuba today presents itself as an unfinished puzzle that must urgently be solved.

A billboard in downtown Havana during the 2008 food crisis reads: "The Absurd First World: Consuming three-quarters of the energy produced in the world."

PART 1

Cuban Agriculture Today:
Realities and Consequences

In part one we describe the socioeconomic, political, climatic and soil characteristics that shape the challenges and opportunities for Cuban agriculture and food security. We also analyze production and consumption patterns, including the impact of food imports and exports from 1998 to 2011. This analysis necessarily takes into account the 1993–1998 period, when Cuba's agricultural policies shifted toward food self-sufficiency, diversification, decentralization and agroecology.

1.1 THE CURRENT NATIONAL AND INTERNATIONAL CONTEXT OF CUBAN AGRICULTURE

From the 15th to the mid-20th century, Cuban agriculture developed in a socioeconomic and political context marked by feudal and semi-feudal colonial regimes, followed by neocolonial capitalism. In 1959, with the triumph of the anti-imperialist guerrilla revolution—led by Fidel Castro Ruz, Ernesto "Che" Guevara, Camilo Cienfuegos and Raúl Castro Ruz—a new chapter in Cuban history began: the establishment of a socialist regime that persists to this day, despite the collapse of Soviet socialism in the late 1980s.

The revolution brought with it two agrarian reform laws to put an end to the abysmal conditions in the Cuban countryside. These laws marked the beginning of an agricultural development model oriented toward the national economy, food security and social well-being.

The First Agrarian Reform Law, passed in 1959, dismantled the large national and foreign-owned landholdings known as *latifundios*. The expropriated lands were used to form a state-owned socialist sector comprising farms and sugarcane cooperatives. The latter at that time occupied 40% of the country's agricultural area. The remaining agricultural area was designated as private landholdings, owned by those who worked the land. The Second Agrarian Reform Law of 1962, however, expanded the role of the state in the agricultural sector, in terms of both land ownership and production, making it the "vital link in the reproduction of national agriculture" (Figueroa 1995, 42).

While the state gained increasing control over the agricultural sector, this did not represent a complete rejection of private land-ownership and non-socialist forms of production. Rather, it was believed that technological progress and agricultural specialization could not be viable within a system of small, privately held farms. Thus, the state opted for a model based on large farms and cooperatives to fully develop the agricultural potential of the country. This view was politically and ideologically reinforced by the First Congress of the Cuban Communist Party (PCC) in its "Tesis y Resoluciones" (1975) on peasants and the agrarian question:

> The dilemma that arises with our peasantry is whether to move to higher, socialist forms of production, or to continue farming small plots in the traditional way, with low yields, low productivity and inefficient use of the land, without compensating for the efforts of individual producers. All this in the midst of a socialist society that is developing through the collective effort of large groups of workers, realizing more and more the achievements of civilization.

Between 1987 and 1992, 82.2% of cultivable lands were part of the state sector. State-owned agricultural enterprises (in sugarcane, rice, potatoes, citrus, fruit and tobacco) and livestock enterprises (primarily beef) were enormous. The average state farm was between 13,000 and 31,000 hectares (32,000 and 76,000 acres). These farms were used to implement large-scale modernization projects modeled on the Green Revolution. This development model gave rise to large monocultures focused on three key export products: tobacco, coffee and sugarcane, which together covered 50% of the country's agricultural land (Funes-Monzote 2009).

Consequently, Cuban agriculture and livestock production became highly dependent on external resources and heavy input use. These resources were provided through the Council for Mutual Economic Assistance (Comecon), an economic organization comprising the Eastern bloc and other communist countries, but above all from the then Union of Soviet Socialist Republics (USSR). The USSR provided the lion's share of Cuba's petroleum, furnished 70% of Cuba's imports and absorbed 85% of Cuban sugar exports. Of course, these were bought and sold at preferential prices that benefited Cuba.

As a result of this relationship, and in the interest of increasing agricultural production for exports and food, Cuba came to use twice the amount of fertilizers per hectare, compared to the United States. Compared to Latin America and the Caribbean, the country's irrigation infrastructure was four times more developed and its level of mechanization twice as high (Sinclair and Thompson 2001). Fertilizer use in Cuba reached levels comparable to European countries. The density of tractors—one for every 50 hectares—was also similar to that of developed countries (Funes-Monzote 2009).

By the late 1970s this model was beginning to show signs of inefficiency due to the massive input requirements, the growing dependence on outside resources and inefficient land use (Nova 2010). To resolve this situation, in 1986 the Cuban government called for the "Rectification of Errors and Negative Tendencies" as an anti-neoliberal and anti-perestroika policy that would increase productive incentives and better link income to production. Already by the late 1980s the cost of Soviet-style agricultural production was far higher than the global average, which translated into increased production costs in Cuba, and in the increased cost of importing intermediate goods, spare parts and fuel.

With the dissolution of the USSR and the socialist camp in 1989, the difficulties affecting Cuba agriculture became both more evident and more pronounced. To make matters worse, the rise to power of the far right in the United States led to an intensification of the blockade that had been imposed since the 1960s. Under these conditions, Cuban agricultural development was brought to a halt by a severe economic crisis. In 1989, the government began to take measures to cope with the possibility of being totally cut off from all external supplies of food, fuel and other inputs. Thus began the era known as the "Special Period in Peacetime."

In the years following the Special Period, a new kind of agricultural development model began to emerge, based upon:

- Diversification (as opposed to monoculture)
- Use of organic means of improving fertility and controlling pests (as opposed to chemicals)
- Turning toward local resources and local development potential (as opposed to external dependence)
- Decentralization of land tenure, markets and decision making (as opposed to centralized control)
- Food self-sufficiency (as opposed to food importation)

As we will see, Cuba continues along this path today, but under new circumstances and new challenges.

Cuban Agriculture in the New Millennium

Due to the effect of fierce competition in the 1990s, the price of grains, dairy, sugar and cooking oil decreased significantly. Given the crisis it was going through, Cuba took advantage of this situation to buy cheap staples on the global market in order to meet domestic demand. However, halfway through the first decade of the new millennium, the situation changed dramatically. Oil prices soared, and food markets were further impacted by agrofuels and speculation.

Between 2003 and 2008, world food prices shot up: rice prices tripled, and maize and wheat prices doubled. The cost of agricultural inputs and transportation also increased. Projections by the Food and Agriculture Organization of the United Nations (FAO 2008) indicate that these prices will remain high until at least 2015, and may never return to below-2004 levels. A 2009 FAO study reported that in Sub-Saharan Africa, 80%–90% of cereals cost 25% more than they had before the crisis, only two years earlier. In Asia, Latin

America and the Caribbean, the prices of 40%–80% of these foods had risen by over 25%.

The impact of these increased prices has been felt most strongly by less-developed countries. In a 2008 report entitled *Double Edged Prices*, Oxfam reported that in South America, where poor families spend up to 70% of their incomes on food, many have had to eat less or settle for less-nutritious foods, in addition to cutting spending on their families' education and health care. Cuba is no exception, since it depends on imports to feed its 11.23 million people, as well as two million tourists annually. In 2007, the island imported US $1.47 billion worth of food. In order to import the same amount of food in 2008, the country had to spend US $2.2 billion, or 50% more than the previous year.

These conditions have created a complicated context for the development of Cuban agriculture. Nonetheless, compared to other countries affected by the crisis, in Cuba the price of the state-subsidized food basket have remained stable. In addition, farmers have

Cuban school children in a rural area

received higher prices as an incentive to increase production. What's more, social spending (on health, education, housing and social security) has continued to grow.

Compared to other countries at the mercy of international organizations like the IMF, World Bank and WTO, Cuba's hands were not tied in dealing with the food crisis. The island maintains its sovereignty and is thus free to make policy changes such as providing land grants to small farmers and co-ops, and incentives to bolster local production as a substitute for expensive imports. All of these measures are due to the fact that the Cuban government sees food as a matter of national security. This means not only satisfying the nutritional needs of the population, but also avoiding external dependence, especially on multinational corporations that control global commodity markets.

Perspectives on the US Blockade

The Torricelli Act of 1992 and the Helms-Burton Act of 1996 led to the resurgence of the United States blockade against Cuba. The laws prohibited any foreign company, including foreign-based American companies, from entering United States ports if it engaged in any commercial trade with Cuba. The goal, of course, was to cut the island off from establishing any trade relations. According to Cuban government estimates, the 50-year blockade has resulted in a total of $90 billion in economic damages. The blockade's tremendously damaging effects have been felt by the entire Cuban population.

The blockade has been condemned by a number of prominent international institutions including the United Nations, which has denounced the blockade for more than 20 years. In 2010, the UN General Assembly voted to oppose the blockade in a vote of 187–2, with three abstentions.

There have been signs of change. Since 2001 the United States has allowed certain companies to sell food to Cuba. President Obama recently stated that the blockade on Cuba makes no sense because it has not been effective in convincing the Cubans of the need for regime change. And in April 2009, the United States government loosened restrictions on the sending of remittances to the island.

New Friends, New Allies, New Opportunities

In spite of these difficulties, Cuba has managed to maintain a foreign policy committed to providing humanitarian aid and solidarity to other countries. Going well beyond so-called disaster relief, Cuba has extended international support in matters of education, culture, health, science and technology. In recognition of Cuba's commitment to international solidarity, many countries throughout the world have shown their support to the Cuban people, sometimes even in defiance of the US blockade.

In November 2008, Cuba's minister of foreign commerce, Raúl de la Nuez, stated that the country maintained trade relations with 176 countries. According to de la Nuez, trade with the Americas had increased, accounting for 53% of trade; trade with Europe made up 22%; and Asia and the Middle East were at 21%. Among Cuba's major trading partners are Venezuela, China, Canada, Spain, Brazil and Vietnam.

In 2004, Venezuela and Cuba formed the Bolivarian Alternative for the Americas (ALBA),[3] an alliance that now has nine member countries. ALBA is not only economic, but also social and cultural in character, and is based on solidarity between member countries. As such, it represents a great opportunity for Cuba, especially in terms of its relationship with Venezuela. According to a recent report by Venezuela's Bank of External Commerce (BANCOEX), Venezuela has signed agreements with Cuba for the operation of five joint ventures in poultry, dairy, vegetables, rice and timber. The two countries also signed an agreement for the production of ethanol, an agrofuel made from sugarcane. Today, many of the island's tractors, owned by state enterprises and cooperatives, operate thanks to these new opportunities, which opened after 2000.

The island is also part of Petrocaribe, a Venezuela-led association established in 2005. With nineteen member countries in the Caribbean, and Central and South America, Petrocaribe was designed to forge cooperation and solidarity in the face of a mounting global

---

[3] At the last ALBA summit, held in Havana in November 2009, the integration initiative was renamed the Bolivarian Alliance for the Americas.

food and fuel crisis. With the help of this alliance, Cuba was able to offset the continuing threat posed by the fluctuating price of oil. Petrocaribe has also expanded its agenda through its anti-hunger project, an initiative that called on the ministries of agriculture of member countries to establish an agricultural fund of $450 million in 2008. Part of the idea was to invest rising oil revenues in agricultural production by improving seeds and fertilizers, plant and animal health, machinery, infrastructure, distribution, marketing and other support services.

In 2000, Cuba was able to join the Southern Common Market (MERCOSUR), which complemented existing bilateral agreements with MERCOSUR countries. In another important symbol of Cuba's integration, the country was recently approved as a member of the Rio Group.

Unlike trade agreements like the Free Trade Area of the Americas (FTAA),[4] Free Trade Agreements (FTAs) and the EU's bilateral agreements, integration plans like ALBA, MERCOSUR and Petrocaribe are based on the principles of fair trade, solidarity and favorable credit terms. Therefore, they run counter to neoliberal rationality, which extols the free market, deregulation and individual profit.

---

[4] The FTAA integration plan, led by the United States, was rejected by most Latin American and Caribbean countries at the Fourth Summit of the Americas, held in 2005 in Mar del Plata, Argentina.

1.2 DEALING WITH CLIMATE CHANGE

Intense Hurricanes

Cuba lends itself to the development of a year-round, diverse agriculture. A popular Cuban saying goes, "Even a pumpkin seed in the middle of the street will grow." But Cuba's geography and geology, as a tropical island, leaves it prone to natural phenomena like hurricanes, which are a constant threat to productivity and agricultural yields.

Over the coming decades, hurricanes are forecast to become more intense. Some have suggested that this is the result of natural cycles of climate variability (Fernández 2005). However, recent research suggests that by increasing ocean-surface temperatures and wind patterns, global climate change will in fact have an impact on hurricane occurrence (BBC 2009).

A peasant farmer does everything in his power to save his taro crop after a hurricane

Prolonged Drought

Another phenomenon threatening the country's agriculture is drought. In recent times, drought periods have become longer due to climate change. Further, prolonged periods of drought followed by intense hurricanes, such as occurred in 2005, can be devastating. It

The Forest Calls the Rain

In "Paraguay," a community on the outskirts of Guantánamo where the air is dry and dusty, even from the road you can see how the soil is covered with a white coat of salt. A tree-farming project was established in that area with the goal of reforesting this very arid region of Guantánamo Province.

Fourteen farms of 30 hectares each participated in the project, six of which were operated by single men. The men were quickly disappointed by the poor results of tree and food production, and left the project. They found the drought and the loneliness too much to bear. Only one farm, number 14, succeeded.

Bonomio and Maria occupied farm number 14. They planted native trees resistant to heat and drought, interspersed with neem and timber trees like cedar, mahogany and hibiscus. "We applied lots of organic matter that we produced ourselves. Mary is an expert at making compost and we captured rainwater through a channel that she built along the roof of our house. When we have more water, life will improve. The forest calls the rain, and the key to our success is that we are here together. With a lot of effort, but also happiness, we have planted a family," says Bonomio.

is estimated that during 2005, production of major crops fell by 36% because of drought, compared to 2004. The phenomenon is felt even more strongly in the eastern provinces, especially in Holguin, Granma, Las Tunas and Guantánamo, where recorded rainfall has been low in recent decades. According to a 2004 report entitled *State of the Cuban Environment*, published by the Ministry of Science, Technology and Environment (CITMA), the western part of the island that year received 81% of its historically recorded rainfall, while the central and eastern regions received only 65% and 62%, respectively. High susceptibility to drought in these regions is one of the factors leading to low development indicators and food insecurity.[5]

Factors That Influence Soil Quality

The poor quality of much of its soil limits Cuba's agricultural potential. Environmental assessments by CITMA and the Ministry of Agriculture (MINAG) have linked the issue of poor soil quality to the most pressing and recurrent ecological problems in Cuba. Most experts agree that Cuban soil degradation is associated with the Green Revolution agricultural model, which focused on the intensive use of chemicals, petroleum and machinery.

Cuba's agricultural land covers an area of 6.6 million hectares, approximately 70% of which suffers some level of degradation. According to a 2006 assessment by The Soil Research Institute, which studied 29 types of crops, 60% of the country's soils, located in 14 of the 15 provinces, are considered unproductive.

A study conducted in 2008 recorded that 45%–60% of Cuban soils lacked organic matter, and 70% suffered from problems due to having 14% salinity and sodicity (high sodium levels), 48.3% erosion and 40.3% acidity (Barreras 2009). The problem of salinity is most pronounced in coastal areas, particularly in the eastern province of Guantánamo, where there are large desertified areas and the average yield is only 30% of historic yields.

---

[5] One mustn't ignore, however, the unequal reach of urban, commercial and industrial development in understanding the regional disparities that exist on the island.

According to Dr. José Febles, a distinguished professor at the Agrarian University of Havana (UNAH), soil erosion in Cuba is significant and its effects are magnified by runoff caused by heavy rains (personal communication, Agrarian University of Havana, January 16, 2008).

The country has made serious efforts to reverse soil degradation. For nearly two decades, it has promoted the increased use of organic fertilizers (compost, humus, mycorrhizae and a wide range of biofertilizers and biostimulants) and green manure to improve the nutritional level of soils and crops. Between 2001 and 2007, national compost production quadrupled, going from four million to 16 million tons. During the same period, vermicompost production increased one million to seven million tons, as reported by Dagoberto Rodríguez, a specialist from the National Soil Conservation and Improvement Program (personal communication, Instituto Nacional de Suelos, Havana, May 8, 2008). Only one year into the implementation of the National Environmental Strategy (2007–2010), CITMA (the Ministry of Science, Technology and Environment's vice minister José Antonio Díaz Duque reported that increased compost production had benefited over half a million hectares. Contour planting is helping to mitigate the effects of soil erosion. At the national level, the annual reforestation plan met 104.9% of its goal, having reforested 55,000 hectares. This has brought the country's total forested area to 25.7% (3.2 million hectares). In 2009, Cuba ranked first in Latin America in forest growth over the past 50 years (Ojeda, 2010).

1.3 AGRICULTURAL PRODUCTION FROM 1993 TO 2009: AN UNSTABLE RECOVERY

As noted above, the current crisis in Cuban agriculture began in the late 1980s when the country lost its access to the inputs necessary to produce enough food. Agricultural and livestock production declined dramatically. Indeed, Cuba's food and economic system was on the verge of total collapse. According to data published by the National Statistics Office (Oficina Nacional de Estadística de Cuba; ONE) in 2004, during the period of 1989–1993, production of tubers decreased by 96%, vegetables by 64%, fruit by 73%, rice by 68%, beans by 62%, cow's milk by 53%, beef by 48% and pork by 52%.

In the face of this crisis, the government made strong adjustments to its agricultural policy in 1993–1994, creating incentives for the recovery and growth of agricultural production. As we will address in part two of this report, the government decentralized and liberalized state-owned lands and promoted nationwide organic agriculture and agroecology.

Thanks to these changes, and to the efforts and innovations of farmers, between 1993 and 1998 the production of numerous products increased: roots and tubers (taro, sweet potatoes and potatoes), vegetables (tomatoes, garlic, onions, peppers and cucumbers) fruit (bananas, plantains, guava, papaya, mango and pineapple) and beans.

The year 1998 marked a critical turning point with production in the main agricultural crops (roots, tubers, fruit and vegetables) growing steadily until 2004 (see graph on page 14). Production declined in 2005, when the island was hit by both drought and powerful hurricanes, but began to show signs of recovery in 2007, when Cuba enjoyed more favorable weather conditions. In 2008, hurricanes hit the island once again, causing losses of $10 billion, mainly in the farm sector.

Between 1998 to 2007, production of starches and tubers (banana, sweet potato, taro and potatoes) increased by 71%, vegetables by 307%, beans by 230%, maize by 209% and fruit by 309%. Growth was also reported in egg production (210%), pork (219%)

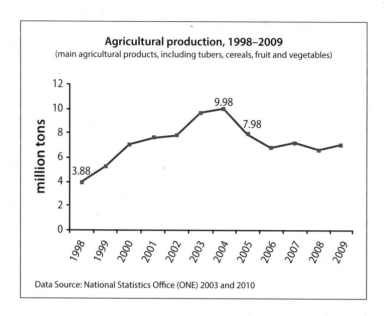

Agricultural production, 1998–2009
(main agricultural products, including tubers, cereals, fruit and vegetables)

Data Source: National Statistics Office (ONE) 2003 and 2010

and mutton and goat (123%). During the same period, however, rice production decreased slightly (1%), and citrus experienced a significant decrease (37%). Fresh milk also decreased by 74%, beef by 73% and poultry by 59%.

Sugar production, which was the traditional engine of the Cuban economy, plummeted beginning in the late 1980s. Between 1995 and 2007, sugar production decreased from 3.2 to 1.15 million tons. This issue will be further analyzed later in this publication.

In general, Cuban agriculture has shown continued growth, while some sectors have declined or been volatile. Experts attribute the latter to the drought and hurricanes of 2005, as well as to national policies that have hindered the development of Cuban agriculture. For example, 30% (two million hectares) of the country's arable land remains uncultivated (Nova 2009). Moreover, the decentralized and participatory agroecological farming systems that since the 1990s have contributed to the sector's recovery still lack the support needed to reach their productive potential. For example, a large amount of food is wasted due to inefficiencies in transportation, processing and storage (Funes-Monzote 2009).

1.4 CUBAN FOOD SECURITY

In Cuba, No One Goes to Bed Hungry

According to FAO data, the number of undernourished people in the world in 2009 was about 840 million. Of this number, 799 million live in developing countries, 30 million in transition countries and 11 million in industrialized countries. By 2003, Cuba had reached the millennium development goals relating to food, as defined by the FAO. Although it continues to face difficulties in food production, and undernutrition[6] and food insecurity is thought to have recently increased, Cuba has achieved the remarkable goal of guaranteeing access to food for its people.

Since the mid-1960s, the Cuban government has regulated the food supply and guaranteed that all Cubans have access to subsidized food. The system operates through a food ration assigned to each person, or through other channels such as meals for the elderly, special meals for children with medical needs, or meals provided in the workplace and schools. Up until the late 1980s, the system of subsidized food rations supplied more than 90% of domestic food consumption.

When the Special Period began, Cuban food consumption underwent a major contraction. During the hardest years of that period (1989–1995), food availability decreased dramatically. Per capita calorie consumption fell to 65.1% of pre-crisis levels, and protein consumption fell to 30%. It is estimated that the average Cuban lost 20 pounds during this period (Sinclair and Thompson 2001). Even under such conditions, every Cuban was able to meet 50%–60% of the daily nutritional requirements through food purchased at subsidized prices, regardless of income or socioeconomic status. Cubans obtained the remainder of their food from hospitals, schools, cafeterias, special programs for vulnerable populations, self-provisioning, state and non-state restaurants, the agricultural market

---

[6] *Undernutrition* means that food intake is not sufficient to consistently meet daily energy requirements.

(state and non-state) and the network of food markets that operate in national or local convertible currencies.

By the year 2000, nutrient intake (calories, proteins and fat) had begun to return to pre-1989 levels (Nova 2006). The availability of food has gradually improved in recent years. In 2005, average daily caloric intake had reached 3,356 calories and 88 grams of protein.

The FAO's 2004 State of Food and Agriculture report states that between 1990 and 2003, the number of undernourished people in Latin America declined from 59.4 to 52.4 million (from 13% to 10% of the population). The report noted that Cuba, Peru and Guyana had already met the millennium development goals in this area, and other countries like Chile and Uruguay were nearing the goal. However, the FAO's 2007 report noted that Cuba had regressed, with an increase in undernutrition from 5% in 2006 to 13% in 2007.

This trend is related to a number of challenges such as the increased cost of food and difficulties in regulating the supply of subsidized food. Other factors to consider are the falling purchasing power of certain sectors, transportation difficulties, market irregularities and poor eating habits of much of the population. However, according to official figures, the risk of undernutrition was less than 2% of the total population in 2007 (Nutrinet 2008).

A number of subsidized food items are currently available including rice, beans, sugar, salt, coffee, chicken, eggs, milk (for children seven years old or younger), potatoes, fish, soy yogurt, meat products (including *picadillo*, ground beef enhanced with soy) and cooking oil. But this system of food distribution has become decreasingly important since the 1980s. In informal conversations, Cuban people estimated that these subsidized foods covered less than a third—seven to ten days—of their monthly food consumption.

In recent years, there has been a diversification of both the foods available and the channels through which people access food. For example, the consumption of vegetables has gradually increased over time. In 1997 the per capita consumption of vegetables was 33 grams per day; by 2000 it had increased to 210 grams per day. It is no longer unusual for Cubans, especially young people, to consume things like radishes, mung beans, chard, spinach, watercress, okra and celery, and fruit such as mamey, cashew apple (*marañón*), canistel, soursop (*guanábana*), passion fruit and pineapple. Increasingly, urban agriculture is meeting the demand for fruits and vegetables as well as contributing to the diversification of urban consumption patterns.

Rural diets have also changed as a result of agricultural and market diversification. For example, farmers of La Palma, Pinar del Rio (in the far western region) have gained tremendous expertise in growing plants for seed. Thanks to these seed banks, they are now able to plant, conserve, improve and consume many different varieties of cassava, beans and corn.

In the face of the economic and food crisis of 2008, Cuba has increased food imports. The government has set in motion an economic adjustment plan that involves restricting electricity consumption, reducing investment in transportation and limiting the amount of food delivered through the national food rationing system. In the second half of 2009, the delivery of beans and peas per person was reduced from 30 to 20 ounces (about 900 to 600 grams), and the usual salt delivery of one kilogram per person every four months was cut in half. By late 2009, Cubans and the Cuban media were predicting a difficult year in 2010, as restrictions on consumption increased and the availability of subsidized food decreased. In April 2011, the Sixth Congress of the Cuban Communist Party recommended the termination of the supplies booklet[7] and the establishment of a differentiated subsidy system.

The problem of food insecurity in Cuba is associated primarily with the economic crisis and the challenges families face in reacting and adapting to the adjustments that are implemented. Studies are being carried out to evaluate specific cases of food insecurity, in order to develop measures tailored to local problems (Aguiloche 2006).

---

[7] Translator's note: The supplies booklet (*libreta de abastecimiento*), created in 1982, establishes the amount and frequency that citizens can access basic food stuffs and supplies at subsidized prices, distributed primarily through local bodegas or convenience stores.

Finally, it must be noted that despite its agricultural problems, in Cuba no one goes to bed without having eaten. Such was the case throughout the difficult years of the 1990s and it remains so today, in the midst of a global food crisis.

An examination of the Cuban food system since 1959 shows us that food security and consumption patterns, in Cuba, as elsewhere, depend not only on increasing food production, but also on the degree to which the state prioritizes these issues and promotes equity in the system of food distribution.

Poor Eating Habits and High Food Prices

According to research conducted in Cuba from 2005 to 2006 on risk factors for health, 24% of adults surveyed did not regularly eat breakfast, 28% regularly cooked with lard and 12% regularly added salt to their food at the table. Furthermore, only about 14% of those surveyed consumed fruits and vegetables daily. Of course, it is widely recognized that poor eating habits are rooted in problems of access to and availability of healthy options.

On the other hand, it has been difficult for Cubans to supplement or improve their diets in view of the upward trend in the free market price of food, which has risen 7.1% since 2005. Cuban consumers access 14% of their protein calories and 28% of their fat calories from the free market. The additional expenses Cubans have had to incur due to rising prices reaches 75% of their total monthly income (Nova 2006).

Although Cuba is largely food secure, undeniably there are segments of the population—focused in certain regions with lower human-development indicators—that remain vulnerable. In contrast, there are families with greater security due to higher income, either from wages or remittances. The four eastern provinces of Las Tunas, Holguín, Guantánamo and Granma are considered the most vulnerable to food insecurity, given their low score on the Human Development Index (HDI). With regard to this situation, one journalist recently commented: "The east has always been in the Special Period."

1.5 IN SEARCH OF IMPORT SUBSTITUTION

Increased Imports

The issue of increased food imports has been the subject of heated debates in Cuba. It is a matter of concern to politicians and academics, farmers and agricultural workers alike. The fact remains that current domestic production is insufficient to feed a population of 11.23 million inhabitants, not counting the two million tourists who visit the island annually. Under these circumstances, imports continue to play an important role in feeding the country.

In 1998, Cuba's food import bill was valued at 704 million pesos. By 2007, the value of imports had risen to 1.47 billion and by 2008, to 2.2 billion. The dramatic increase between 2007 and 2008 is mainly associated with the price hikes of the global food crisis. A 2011 report calculated that, 25% more would be spent on food imports than the year before (EFE 2011).

Over the period of 1998 to 2009, the percentage of food imported by Cuba increased by 112%. By 2009, half of the food consumed in

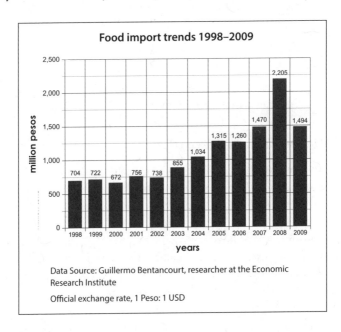

Food import trends 1998–2009

Data Source: Guillermo Bentancourt, researcher at the Economic Research Institute

Official exchange rate, 1 Peso: 1 USD

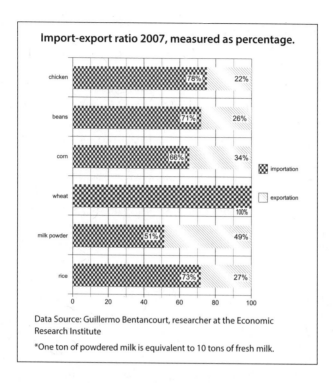

Import-export ratio 2007, measured as percentage.

Data Source: Guillermo Bentancourt, researcher at the Economic Research Institute

*One ton of powdered milk is equivalent to 10 tons of fresh milk.

Cuba was imported. However, increased spending on food imports has not necessarily meant an increase in the amount of food imported. Rather, increased spending is due to the rising price of agricultural products and transportation, both magnified by rising oil prices.

Food Imports from the United States

In October 2000, the US Congress passed the Trade Sanctions Reform and Export Enhancement Act, which led to an increase in United States exports to Cuba. The measure allowed United States companies to sell food and medicine to Cuba for humanitarian reasons. Thus, after Hurricane Michelle hit the island in 2001, the United States began to sell food and agricultural products to Cuba in December of that year, with payments and shipping done through third-party countries. In that year alone, Cuba spent 4.3 million USD on United States goods.

Some of the most important foods imported from the United States are corn, wheat, chicken, soybeans and soybean products, rice and powdered milk, all of which are foods widely consumed by the population and accessed through the supplies booklet (Pérez 2009).

Researchers at the Center for the Study of the Cuban Economy (CEEC) express differing views on the significance of rising imports of United States goods. García (2007) argues that these imports represent a threat inasmuch as they disrupt domestic sectors, such as poultry production, and could ultimately undermine domestic producers. By contrast, Pérez (2009) notes that if relations between the two countries improved, Cuba could improve its financial position while giving a small boost to farmers in the United States during its recession.

In 2007, food imports from the United States were valued at 438 million USD, representing 30% of total food imports. According to the United States-Cuba Trade and Economic Council, the value of imports from the United States had increased to 528 million USD in 2009. However, the council's 2011 report shows a 31% decrease to 366 million USD in 2010.

In any country, increasing food imports invariably has an impact on local production, primarily that of small farmers and peasants. Such was the case with Mexican tortillas, for example. As a result of the United States flooding the Mexican market with cheap corn (a practice known as "dumping") between 1989 and 2003, the real domestic price of corn dropped by 50%. Furthermore, over a 20-year period, the purchasing power of rural incomes dropped to one third of its original level. In Mexico and throughout the Global South, many small farmers have had no choice but to leave the countryside for the cities in search of work.

This has not happened in Cuba because government regulations prevent imports from competing directly in local markets. Nonetheless, importing food necessarily diverts resources and attention away from local production, which indirectly affects local market dynamics. In addition, many foods that are imported could be produced domestically. Researchers at CEEC, for instance, have assessed the country's ability to produce staple foods such as rice, beans and milk at an affordable cost.

"Popular rice": Reconciling Price, Technology and Soils

Cubans consume about 600,000 tons of rice annually, but national rice production has been able to meet only a fraction of this demand. At the highest point, in 1988, Cuba produced 250,000 tons of rice, using conventional high-input methods. In the 1990s, national rice production never exceeded 80,000 tons annually.

In 1994, in both rural and urban areas, a movement emerged in which people began planting rice everywhere they could, especially on marginal lands such as roadsides. Within just four years, the production of "popular rice" surpassed the production of "specialized" rice by 100 tons, or 16%.

As a result, the state began granting support to popular-rice growing in the form of technical advice and other resources. In 2008, government officials suggested popular rice be renamed "nonspecialized rice." However, José A. Díaz Luque, vice minister of Science, Technology and Environment (CITMA) points out that rice is a highly technical crop requiring high levels of inputs, crop management, mechanization and postharvest care. He also notes that it is important to continue increasing production without compromising the environment, the integrity of organic methods or the purchase price paid to farmers.

Fortunately, there is already a plan in Cuba to promote import substitution, that includes various institutions involved in food production and distribution. In a report presented in April 2008, the Ministry of Foreign Commerce (MINCEX) stated the plan was yielding positive results, but had yet to overcome a number of issues including the inability of farmers to distribute their products to consumers; interruptions in the supply of raw materials due to lack of funding; investment delays; and contract inefficiencies.

Thus, the substitution of imported food remains an important agricultural, social and political challenge for the Cuban people. The country's external vulnerability makes overcoming dependence critical, and Cuba possesses many resources that have not been fully developed their, including large expanses of uncultivated land, a highly educated population and innovative small farmers.

1.6 CUBAN AGRICULTURAL EXPORTS: CHANGES AND PROSPECTS

Agricultural and Raw Material Exports

Before the fall of the Soviet Union, sugar and non-food agricultural exports were Cuba's main source of foreign exchange, representing around 80% of total exports. This in turn financed the country's food imports. But these exports have declined in recent years, dropping by 35% between 1999 and 2007.

Between 2003 and 2007, nickel rose to the top of the export list, due to a significant increase in the price of the mineral on the world market. In 2007 Cuba produced nearly 76,000 tons of nickel, valued at $2.7 billion. One year later, however, the global crisis created a collapse in nickel prices, causing it to drop to one-sixth of that value. This had a severe impact on the Cuban economy.

Cuba's second most important export in 2007 was medicine and medical equipment, valued at $289 million in 2007 (compared to $306 million in 2006). In third place was tobacco, valued at $245.9 million in 2006, and $236.3 million in 2007. Finally, in fourth place, sugar was exported at a value of $215 million in 2006, and fell to $193 million in 2007. This is a significant drop considering that sugar and sugar-derived products represented more than 70% of the total value of exported goods in the 1970s and 1980s; by 2006, sugar products made up less than 8% of exports (Nova 2006).

Exports of Products and Services

Cuba has transitioned from an economic model based on the export of raw materials to one focused primarily on the service sector. For example, in the case of tourism alone, services contributed $0.2 billion to Gross Domestic Product (GDP) in 1994, and $2 billion in 2004. The most economically important service sectors in Cuba are tourism and medicine, but other sectors are also important, including education, culture, athletics, high technology and, to a lesser extent, agriculture. At the end of 2005, the service sector accounted for 70% of GDP (Funes-Monzote 2008).

In 2007, the government reported that the service sector had grown dramatically for the third consecutive year, reaching $8.36 billion, double its 2004 value. Thanks to the increase in income from services, mainly driven by exports to Venezuela, Cuba was able to balance its external finances despite a trade deficit.

According to researchers from the Government Statistics Committee, exports of both nickel and pharmaceutical products remain critical to the economy for the time being. Meanwhile, Cuba's service economy holds great potential, mainly due to its wealth of human capital, as well as international prestige garnered from its rapid social progress.

In short, the last few years have seen Cuba's domestic production and import-export structure undergo important transformations that form the context for its current push to diversify the economy, develop the country's resources and promote food security. Meeting these goals will require strengthening new organizational spaces to meet the challenges posed by new economic circumstances.

"Popular rice" as a substitute for imported foods

PART 2

Current Cuban Agricultural Policies: The Challenge of Being Unique

In part two we address Cuba's current agricultural policies, focusing on the elements that make the country so unique. We also analyze the challenges the island faces in the wake of the transformation begun in the 1990s, concerning land tenure, the domestic market, the cooperative sector, labor shortages, agribusiness in the sugarcane sector, organic production standards and certification, and genetically modified (GM) crops. Finally, we describe the new policy strategy that has emerged in the 21st century.

2.1 THE URGENCY OF CHANGE

As already mentioned, in the 1980s the Cuban economy, and agriculture in particular, went into a deep crisis caused by both an inefficient agricultural model and the sudden halt of outside resources entering the country.

Within Cuba there are two schools of thought regarding the crisis. One view attributes the crisis to the fall of the socialist bloc and the demise of the USSR, thus identifying the origins of the crisis as *external* to the Cuban system. The other view attributes the crisis almost exclusively to *internal* factors related to dysfunctions within the system (Sánchez and Triana 2008).

It is important to note that the pre-1989 agricultural model—while ensuring an adequate level of food consumption—had many negative environmental impacts, such as land degradation, deforestation, water pollution and the reduction of biodiversity. These impacts have been well documented by the Ministry of Science, Technology, and Environment (CITMA) in its 1997 report *Environmental Strategy of the Republic of Cuba.*

In 1985, the government began openly acknowledging the problems associated with its development model, and in 1986 it embarked upon a strategy called the "rectification of errors and negative tendencies." This process consisted of addressing the mistakes made in a number of areas, such as economic planning and administrative structures, as well as agricultural production and markets (Castro 1985). It was in this context that the state made changes to its agricultural policy in 1993. The changes sought to build on endogenous resources to reinvigorate the agricultural sector, increase production and agricultural incomes, and resolve the problems emerging in Cuba's ongoing transformation (Pérez Villanueva 2000).

2.2 CHANGES IN LAND TENURE: 1993 TO 2009

The 1960s Land Reform: Precursors, Singularity and Repercussions in Latin America

Prior to 1959, property and land tenure were highly concentrated in *latifundios*, enormous sugarcane plantations and ranches. Twenty-five percent of the land was in the hands of foreign capital, mainly American, "while the national bourgeoisie monopolized another twenty percent" (Valdés Paz 2005a, 22). These *latifundios* owned 95% of the farms over 402 hectares (Valdés Paz 2005b, 10). The National Statistics Office (ONE) estimates that in 1957, 9.4% of landowners owned 73% of the country's land, indicating a highly unequal distribution of productive resources in the agricultural sector (Nova 2006).

The revolution of 1959 opened a new chapter in Cuban history with the decree of the First Agrarian Reform Law in May 1959, which focused on two key objectives: the dismantling of latufundios, and the redistribution of land among peasants, agricultural workers and anyone who demonstrated knowledge of farming. The Second Agrarian Reform Law of 1963 nationalized farms of more than 67 hectares (about 145 acres), with some exceptions. These reform laws resulted in a dual land-tenure structure, with 50% of the agricultural land owned by the state and 50% by the private sector.

However, in the following years the state began expanding its landholdings, as farmers decided to sell their lands to the state for various reasons. In addition to payment for their lands, sellers also received a retirement pension from the state. As a result, by the 1980s the state owned 80%–82% of the land, with the remaining held by the private sector. State lands would later be redistributed once more, not in response to popular demands, but rather as part of a strategy to boost agricultural development.

The Cuban Agrarian Reform Project had great global repercussions, particularly in Latin America, where it inspired similar processes. The Cuban example continues as a paradigm of "giving the land to the tiller," accompanied by policies to improve well-being in

TABLE 1. Cuban agrarian reform compared to other Latin American agrarian reforms of the 20th century

Characteristics	Cuba	Brazil, Columbia, Dominican Republic , Ecuador, Honduras, Paraguay and Venezuela
Beneficiaries	Farmers and the rural poor	Multinational corporations, and national landowners and agribusinesses
Landownership	State ownership	Mostly sponsored by the US through the "Alliance for Progress," with the goal of creating a class of middle-sized (private) farmers, to act as a buffer between peasants and the large industrial sector
Access to credit, education, employment, health, housing- and market-access subsidies, social security	The state guarantees and subsidizes social welfare, guided by the principle of social equity	The state is unable to guarantee access to social services; the majority of peasant families remain below the poverty line
Link between the rural and peasant populations with the national development strategy	Peasants play an important role both as food producers and consumers	Peasants are excluded from the national economy; in addition, they are harmed by the dumping of foreign agricultural products in local markets
Technological model	Adoption of an agro-ecological model based on low external inputs, with ecological pest control and organic fertilization	Industrial model based on monocultures and high external- and chemical-input use
On a path to food security and food sovereignty	Reforms grounded in the human right to food, and sovereign decision making over the country's food system	High rural food insecurity and limited ability to make sovereign decisions about food and agriculture policies

Based on data obtained from Arruda 2007; Rosset 2007

the country through access to health, education, housing, electricity, drinking water, recreation, culture and social security. These factors make the standard of living in the Cuban countryside one of the highest in the Americas.

The Great Cooperative Expansion of 1993

Prior to 1993, the state agricultural sector comprised state-owned enterprises (sugarcane, fruit, citrus, tobacco, coffee, cocoa, rice, pork, beef, poultry, etc.), in addition to the Youth Labor Army (EJT) and urban gardens used by labor centers for self-provisioning. The non-state sector consisted of the Agricultural Production Cooperative (CPA) and Credit and Service Cooperative (CCS), as well as individual peasants, who possessed private land titles or permanent, nontransferable usufruct titles.[8]

The CPAs were formed by farmers who voluntarily came together to collectivize their lands and their work organization. The CCSs, by contrast, were formed by peasants in order to access credit and services, while maintaining their individual, private lands.

Beginning in 1993, the cooperative sector began to expand. That year saw the most important transformations in land tenure since the passage of the Second Agrarian Reform Law. This transformation consisted in the redistribution of 60% of state lands to groups of workers to work the lands in usufruct. The Basic Units of Cooperative Production (UBPC) emerged from this transformation, which, because of its scale and strategic importance, is now known as the Third Agrarian Reform.

By 2007, the UBPCs already controlled 37% of all agricultural lands. There are UBPCs of all sizes, from a UBPC *organopónico*[9]

---

[8] The Cuban Constitution affirms the legal statues of agricultural cooperatives and farmers' rights to associate in cooperatives.

[9] Translator's note: *Organopónicos* are small-scale organic gardens. First officially established in 1991 in the effort to promote self-sufficiency during crisis, *organopónicos* have since become the model for the majority of Cuba's urban gardens.

of less than one hectare, to a livestock UBPC of 2,000 hectares. However, it is critical to note that the state did not embark on a full-scale privatization of land, as happened in many countries under neoliberal adjustments driven by the World Bank and IMF. In Cuba, the state redistributed cooperative and decentralized landholdings and land management, but not ownership.

Cuba has followed a unique path for land redistribution. The most recent land reforms have led to an increased dominance of the private, cooperative and usufruct sectors, as shown in the charts below.

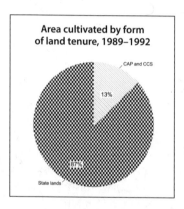

Area cultivated by form of land tenure, 1989–1992

CAP and CCS — 13%
State lands — 87%

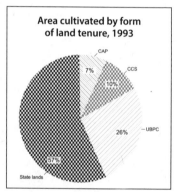

Area cultivated by form of land tenure, 1993

CAP — 7%
CCS — 10%
UBPC — 26%
State lands — 57%

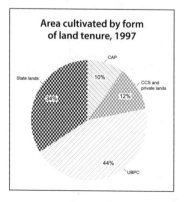

Area cultivated by form of land tenure, 1997

CAP — 10%
CCS and private lands — 12%
State lands — 34%
UBPC — 44%

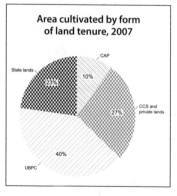

Area cultivated by form of land tenure, 2007

CAP — 10%
CCS and private lands — 27%
State lands — 23%
UBPC — 40%

Distribution of Idle Lands: Applications and Results

Orlando Ortega Delgado and Maria Josefa Gonzalez, farmers in the municipality of La Palma, Pinar del Rio, argue that "there's a lot of idle land around here and a lot of people who want land." José Antoni from the Provincial Directorate of Statistics in Sancti Spiritus comments, "Some people have land with only a few cows grazing on it that isn't reported as idle, but it's obviously underutilized. This doesn't happen in the private sector."

In July 2007, current president Raúl Castro Ruz publicly stated that 51% of the agricultural lands in the country were vacant or unoccupied. Thus, he announced that land would be handed over in usufruct to anyone who had the will, ability and resources to produce on them immediately. The announcement was widely welcomed by farmers, agricultural workers and Cuban citizens in general. There followed a series of consultations with peasants, workers, women, professionals, agronomists, institutions and people's organizations from across the country.

In September 2008, Decree 259 was enacted, providing land grants to anyone with the skills and resources required to make them immediately productive. This decree opened the door for arable lands to be owned not only by state agencies and cooperatives, but also by all eligible individuals with the physical capacity and qualifications for farming.

The decree stipulates that applicants who do not own land can receive up to 13.42 hectares (about 33 acres), and those who already have land in full production may receive up to 40.26 hectares (about 99 acres). Individuals may receive land for a period of 10 years, renewable for 25 years. The usufruct land is nontransferable and therefore cannot be sold to a third party. Under exceptional circumstances in which a landowner is no longer able to work the land, he or she may terminate the application and recommend another individual who has already been working the land over an extended period.

Looking at the evolution of land distribution programs over time, one notes a continual commitment to social justice in the agrarian reform laws of both 1959 and 1963. Decree 259 of 2008 is thus an extension of the same philosophy of "land to the tiller" that is at the heart of Cuban socialism.

According to the Ministry of Agriculture (MINAG) data, by October 20, 2008, Decree 259 (also known as Resolution 688/2008) had distributed 69,086 land grants, broken down into the following land uses: cattle, 41.7%; mixed crops, 40.9%; small livestock, 7.7%; rice, 6.5%; coffee, 1.6%; tobacco, 1.5%; and sugarcane, 0.2%. As these statistics show, the majority of land requests were for cattle, crops and small livestock. This is due to new incentives that have made these activities attractive in recent years, and also to their importance in meeting domestic food needs.

The low number of requests for planting sugarcane is explained by the difficulties in this sector beginning in the 1980s, in addition to, as we shall see below, the state-led restructuring of the agricultural sector in the second half of the 20th century. This data shows that the redistribution of land tenure and land management has not favored export crops, but rather activities that contribute to the country's food security. In essence, food production for domestic consumption has become a priority.

Between 2009 and 2011, 41% to 63% of idle land was distributed, accounting for 7% of the national agricultural area, of which 24%

Now that milk fetches a good price, dairy farmer Orlando requested land to grow sugarcane or king grass for fodder

is in cultivation. Ninety-eight percent of land requests came from individuals, 79% came from landless individuals, 70% came from individuals with no previous experience in agriculture, and more than 80% are now concentrated in Credit and Service Cooperatives (CCSs) and Strengthened Credit and Service Cooperatives (CCSFs) (Ministerio de Economía 2008; Gonzalez 2009; Varela Pérez 2011). The central report approved at the Sixth Congress of the Cuban Communist Party in April 2011 officially recognized that there is still much land left to cultivate.

Referring to the land distributions before 1993, Cuban sociologist Juan Valdés Paz (2005a, 169) once commented: "This process of creating new individual producers, this repeasantization, could be extended to all qualified applicants and to all of the available lands." Decree 259 moves in that direction. With the broad-ranging distribution of lands there is now real opportunity for large numbers of individuals, families and communities to live and work in the countryside. As new farmers, they carry on the legacy of traditional agricultural practices, such as the sustainable management of agroecosystems, ensuring optimum yields and ecological resilience. Indeed, there are growing incentives, including higher incomes, available to people in the countryside. People who had once abandoned agriculture are now returning to it.

Of the institutional requests for land, the majority (56%) came from CCSFs. While this data is preliminary, it points to a strengthening of the cooperative model. What's more, new individual landholders also tend to join cooperatives, further promoting this trend. Indeed, the decree regulations encourage new landowners to associate themselves with cooperatives and to negotiate with the state through the cooperative system. In this respect, Article 22 of Chapter IV, Article 282 of Decree 259, explicitly states:

> The products and revenues obtained by purchase or sale of tools, equipment, agricultural inputs and livestock, accrued to the usufructuary, will be performed in accordance with the standards established by the CCS with which they are associated, or another identified person (Official Gazette of the Republic of Cuba 2008).

TABLE 2. Land distributions, 1959–2008

Land Distributions, 1959–2008	Main Goals	Results
1959: First Agrarian Reform Law	Meet the demands of peasants and agricultural workers	Distribution of one million hectares to tenant farmers and squatters; the private sector came to occupy 39% of the country's total area and 50% of the agricultural land
1963: Second Agrarian Reform Law	Nationalize lands held by the oligarchy and US corporations	Between 1963 and 1988, state-owned properties increased from 60% to 82%
1991: Decree 125, regulating the possession, ownership and inheritance of land and agricultural assets	Develop and promote export production (coffee, cacao, tobacco and other crops)	By 1998, the state had distributed 101,588 hectares in usufruct to urban and semi-urban landholders: • 54,806 hectares for coffee, to 12,719 beneficiaries (avg. of 4.3 hectares each) • 41,602 hectares for tobacco, to 20,891 beneficiaries (avg. of 2 hectares each) • 5,180 hectares for other crops, to 22,876 beneficiaries (avg. 0.23 hectares each)
1993: Decree 142, regulating the creation of Basic Cooperative Production Units (UBPCs)	Decentralize, liberalize and redistribute state-owned lands	28.5% of the country's total area, 42% of its agricultural land and 47.6% of its cultivated land become Basic Units of Cooperative Production (UBPCs)
2008: Law 259, regulating the distribution of idle lands	Distribute state-owned lands, in usufruct, to CCSs, CPAs and UBPCs	Between 2008 and 2009 more than 700,000 hectares of vacant land, representing 40% of all idle lands, were distributed

Data Sources: Valdés Paz 2006; Nova 2006; author interview with Adolfo Alvarado Esquijarosa (ANAP); and statistics from ACTAF

In summary, Cuba's key land redistribution policies were carried out in 1959, 1963, 1993 and 2008 according to different objectives. In 1959, land was distributed in response to the political demands for land by farmers and agricultural workers who worked or squatted on large estates before the revolution. While it did not refer explicitly to distribution, the Second Agrarian Reform Law laid out the need to expropriate large and foreign landholdings that had been bypassed by the First Agrarian Reform Law, implying a transfer of these lands to the state. State land distributions carried out beginning in the 1970s—including Decree 259 in 2008—responded to the need for economic and agricultural development.

Challenges Ahead

A unique aspect of the Cuban experience is decision-making power, such as land-management decisions, at the local level. The responsibility of decision making has posed a great challenge for local authorities, as it has required them to evaluate requests and identify potential problems. For example, there have been cases in which two or more parties have applied for the same land, requested land outside the allotted territory, or requested new land while already possessing uncultivated lands. Consequently, in some places the process has been very slow.

Another important challenge is accessing the resources needed to work the land; this is the Achilles heel of modern Cuban agriculture. The words of peasant farmer Vestina Ardaz Mederos illustrate the point: "There is no way to acquire the minimum necessary resources for work on the farm. There are no stores where you can buy what you need; even something as simple as a rope for securing the animals is very difficult to obtain (personal communication, La Palma, Pinar del Río, Cuba, July 27, 2008)." Another farmer, Roberto de Dìos Suàrez, confessed, "Yes, there are problems here. I have to work with the small amount of fuel that I'm able to buy on the sly. I have a plan, but no inputs, so I have to do something. It pains me to say it, but sometimes I have no choice but to buy what someone is selling out here, which may be stolen from the state. It's the only way to produce food for the people. They promise us this or that, but the resources never come. There are no inputs at all" (personal communication, Guantanamo, Cuba, August 16, 2008).

It is widely understood that land distributions, while necessary and timely, are not sufficient to solve the country's agricultural problems. Many other elements are needed, such as secure tenure, market incentives (credit, price supports, etc.), storage infrastructure, distribution and marketing support, and input subsidies.

The provinces are now making great efforts to solve the problem of providing resources for producers. The role of state agricultural enterprises[10] is also changing. According to Miguel Torres Hernández, director of the Municipal Agricultural Supply and Transport Company in Sancti Spiritus, the role of the company has changed from one of allocating resources to taking requests to help producers find the resources they need. Since October 2008, each producer receives a subsidy of 0.18 cents CUC (Cuban Convertible Peso) for each quintal (100 pounds) he or she delivers, which the producer can use to buy inputs in a local store. Previously, this system applied only to a few high-priority or export crops. Today, it applies to all crops.

---

[10] Translator's note: State agricultural enterprises include all farming, supply, coordination and distribution enterprises run by the state directly. Some of the crops that are still cultivated in state farms are citrus, tobacco, coffee, rice, etc.; however, the role of the state in the farming sector has declined and, as described above, its role in resource allocation and coordination continues to evolve as well.

2.3 CUBA, A COUNTRY OF COOPERATIVES

The Strengthened Credit and Service Cooperatives (CCSFs)

Since 1998, the state has promoted what it calls "Strengthened CCSs" (CCSFs) with the objective of increasing the local capacity for management, social benefits and production.

In general, peasant farmers view the strengthening of credit and service cooperatives in a positive light, considering this an opportunity to improve their production and income.

In a 2006 interview with the newspaper *Granma*, ANAP (Asociación Nacional de Agricultores Pequeños—National Small

---

The Credit and Service Cooperatives Get Organized

Placencia Zoila Lopez is the chair of the board of directors of the Strengthened Credit and Service Cooperative (CCSF). She is an expert farmer and innovator in food conservation and processing. Established March 20, 1998, CCSF is the first of its kind in San Andrés, La Palma, Pinar del Río. When asked about the co-operative's accomplishments, the chairwoman comments: "The board is in charge of operations, so the farmer does not have to leave the valley. We deliver the requested resources directly to the farmers. They  also no longer have to wait for the State Collection Agency to come and collect their produce, and they receive payments much faster."

In five years this CCSF succeeded in settling its bank debts, incurred for the purchase of a tractor, truck and other items, which are now assets of the cooperative. Decisions are made in the assembly, with the participation and vote of all members. Members of the board of directors are compensated according to the co-op's profit margin.

Farmers Association) president Orlando Lugo Fonte declared, "As a whole, the CPAs, the CCSs and the individual producers, which possess 37% of the country's agricultural land, contribute about sixty percent the of tubers, vegetables, beans and pork" (Funes-Monzote 2009:36). Recent data confirms that peasant farmers produce 60% of the meat and vegetables, 96% of the tobacco, 70% of the pork, 62% of the beef, 59% of the cow's milk and 90% of the small livestock (Funes-Monzote 2009; see appendix 1 for more detail). These statistics demonstrate the productive potential of peasant producers, and explain why the state is working to strengthen the peasant sector as a whole, and in particular the CCSs.

Between 1996 and 2007, according to official statistics, the landholdings of cooperatives increased 9.5%, while the landholdings of individual farmers and sharecroppers increased by 4.8%.

Data for 2008 indicate that these cooperatives and individual producers are the most productive Cuban farmers, a fact that is reflected in their income statistics. Between 1994 and 2004, cooperative monthly earnings rose from 209 to 1,139 pesos, representing a growth of 445%. For their part, individual producers reached monthly income levels of more than 1,714 pesos in 2004 (ONE 2007). In Cuba, farmers receive the highest incomes of anyone working in the legal economy.[11]

---

[11] According to figures provided by the government of Fidel Castro Ruz, on April 21, 2005, the minimum wage was raised to 225 pesos, ratified by Resolution 11/2005 of the Ministry of Labor. In 2006, the ministry announced that the average monthly wage of workers was 282 Cuban pesos, equivalent to 11.28 CUC (convertible currency unit), based on the current Cuban exchange rate. In 2007, the average salary was 408 pesos (16.3 CUC). Twenty-five Cuban pesos equals one CUC; one CUC is equivalent to 1.08 USD.

The Agricultural Production Cooperatives (CPAs), Overcoming Difficulties

Between 1996 and 2007, production levels in CPAs essentially stagnated due a number of factors, such as aging members and a lack of incentives. Currently, 20% of all CPA members are retired or on the verge of retiring (ANAP 2006). ONE reports that monthly income figures from CPAs rose from 151 to 264 pesos in 10 years (from 1994 to 2004), representing a growth of 75%. This is far less than that of CCSs, which grew by 445% between 1994 and 2004.

Farmers believe that the problems facing CPAs—lack of resources and labor—require the implementation of more efficient production systems.

In fact, some CPAs have taken steps toward a more diversified, efficient model, without sacrificing social benefits. For example, the "Camilo Cienfuegos" CPA, located in the municipality of Bahía Honda, Pinar del Rio, provides housing for workers and their families in modern buildings, in addition to a community center and senior center, all on the cooperative grounds. In addition to sugarcane, the CPA has now been diversified to produce rice, milk, freshwater fish and other products, which are sold at "fixed prices"[12] to members and the community.

The Recovery of the Basic Units of Cooperative Production (UBPCs)

Since the late 1990s, and especially since 2000, the difficulties faced by the Basic Units of Cooperative Production (UBPCs), formerly state farms, have become an important topic of discussion. Since their inception in 1993, UBPCs have not lived up to expectations. Studies conducted between 2001 and 2007 show how UBPC output has diminished over time, and how most are not profitable.

UBPC revenues increased from 581 to 675 pesos between 2000 and 2004, a 16% growth, according to ONE. The CPAs reported similarly poor revenue levels. The poor performance of both UBPCs

---

[12] "Fixed price" products are sold at a higher price than in the state-regulated market, but always less than the free market price.

and CPAs is due in part to their limited access to supply and demand markets, in addition to the insufficient support for home consumption, housing and health care.

A widely held view is that the autonomy of UBPCs is undermined by excessive dependency on, and control by, the state enterprise from which they emerged. Research conducted by the Cuban sociologist Niurka Pérez Rojas betwen 1994 to 2003 demonstrated that "Worker participation based on the criterion of management autonomy became increasingly difficult due to the excessive supervision that state enterprises exercised over UBPCs. Their members have demanded the right to decide matters of importance to the collective, both within their units and in national meetings. Generally speaking, the state enterprises intervene and have the major weight in strategic decisions (drawing up plans, distribution and control of energy and fertilizers, beginning and end of harvest, investments, etc.), and the UBPCs have decision-making power over how they use their materials" (Rojas and Echevarría 2006). The UBPCs bear the burden of heavy bank debts, lack of farming inputs such as fertilizers and pesticides, and the devaluated assets of their "mother company" (state enterprise). These entities are made up of workers who were required by decree, not of their own volition, to form cooperatives. To make matters worse, the "mother company" to which they were subordinated manages them in a bureaucratic style. All of these problems make it very difficult, if not impossible, to recruit and retain an adequate workforce.

However, using 39.87% of Cuba's farmland, the UBPCs should play an important role in the country's food production. As such, the state has not given up on the UBPCs and has even shown an increased willingness to rescue them. Beginning in 2004, for example, new regulations were put in place to decentralize UBPCs and improve their cooperative management. The following year, in 2005, the government created a specific deputy minister position within MINAG to oversee UBPCs. In addition, UBPCs received financial assistance of up to 135.6 million pesos between 2002 and 2006 (ONE 2008).

In view of the Cuban government's current land-distribution policies, the percentage of land in the hands of UBPCs is likely to continue its gradual decline in the coming decades. Perhaps this process will lead to a positive transformation of these entities.

In recent years, successful UBPCs have been identified, and they are now serving as model for others. In the model UBPCs, the workers are less like wage laborers and more like partners: they are responsible for their own farms or plots, make their own decisions and are free to use either unpaid family labor or hired wage labor based on their needs. Each farmer establishes a contractual relationship with the management and fellow cooperative members. One of the most successful UBPCs, called "The Mango," is located in San Cristobal, Pinar del Río. Its manager, Nardo Bobadilla, reveals the secret to his success: "The independence of the company; the sense of autonomy and ownership, and democratic decision making; and the support for workers, families and communities."

Similar statements were recorded in "La Miriam" (also known as "Los Guerrilleros"), another successful UBPC in the municipality of La Palma. There, each worker works his or her own piece of land, with the help of family or hired labor. Carmelo Pérez Martínez, the UBPC's manager, stresses that the work they do aims to improve overall economic well-being: 50% of all profits are distributed among the members. In the UBPC's first year in 1994, members received an average of 150 pesos per month. In July 2008, they expected a payment of 715 pesos.

As is often the case, one of the UBPC's top social welfare priorities is housing. Consequently, thirteen houses were being built, with materials provided by the state beginning in 2007. Moreover, the granting of credit to workers creates a good economic stimulus. "My workers' bank is me," says Carmelo (Chan 2008).

In the "Jobo Rosado" UBPC, workers say quality of life has greatly improved since the average income per member increased, by 20% in 2005, and by 60% in 2007. The key to success for this organization has been increased production, yields and sales; on-farm cost centers; family health care; and profit sharing.

Another successful UBPC, located in the urban area of Alamar, Habana del Este, Havana City, is not controlled by a company, and manages currency independently. The Alamar UBPC is seen as an example that could spread to others. Indeed, Luis Pi Leon, manager of the "Grito de Baire" UBPC comments, "Alamar UBPC is our future."

The official plan to rescue the UBPCs and strengthen the CPAs and CCSs is summarized succinctly by an important scholar of Cuban agrarian reform: "The success of the Cuban cooperative system today is not a question of feasibility, but rather of political will" (Burchardt 2000).

2.4 MARKETS AND EQUITY IN THE AGRICULTURAL SECTOR

New Marketing Channels for Producers

In Cuba, since the 1990s there has been a free market with prices governed by the logic of supply and demand, but in a manner completely different from the neoliberal model. Unlike neoliberalism, the socialist state assumed the responsibility of protecting producers and consumers from extreme price fluctuations, and ensuring that access to high-quality products was not limited only to affluent members of society.

Before 1993, the state market dominated the economy. And although a free market space was created in the early 1980s, it was abolished in 1986 because of the speculation it generated. Finally, in 1994, the free market was reopened, with little interference from the state until 2008, when it intervened to reduce food prices.

It must be said that the state's ability to compete in the free market while maintaining a consistent supply, in quantity or quality, is limited. The ration market, however, in which the state delivers food at subsidized prices, has been reliable over the years.

In the free market and "sale points" (*puntos de venta*), which will be discussed below, the supply is stable, but the prices are high. Consequently, the free market has had greater relevance and presence in the cities, especially in the capital. In the interior of the

A good day at the Sunday market

"Punto de venta" (sale point) of Nikoyin, a
Cuban of Japanese ancestry

country, especially in rural and suburban areas, these markets have
a weaker presence, since people can more easily access food directly
from producers without going through intermediaries.

For intermediaries, both legal and illegal, it is more attractive to
sell in urban markets, where consumers are generally able to pay a
higher price. It is common to see producers and middlemen trans-
porting their goods to urban centers. Trucks full of fruits and tubers
from as far away as the eastern provinces reach Havana's markets
and sale points, where they sell at high prices. Thus, it was necessary
for the state to take steps to ensure that local produce didn't travel
excessive distances. For example, the state discouraged cooperatives
from selling their products far away when local demand was great,
and allowed local prices to be adjusted to reflect supply and demand.

Another marketing channel that emerged after 1993 was the
"sale points" (*puntos de venta*), similar to the US's "fruit stands." This
form of marketing was briefly shut down between the summer of
2007 and early 2008 due to disorder and illegal conduct. There had
been small sale points throughout the island. In some cases, two

sale points owned by the same cooperative were found operating on the same block. It is estimated that there were 14,000 sale points across the country, most concentrated in Havana Province. In late 2008, following the hurricanes and the spike in fuel prices, price speculation in the open market spiraled out of control. It is not known exactly how many sale points were closed for violations, but in Havana Province, the decline was noticeable. It remains to be seen how the system of sale points will adjust to market changes in coming years.

The Conflict Between Farmers and the State Collection Agency

Since the 1990s, there have been constant complaints from peasant producers about the State Collection Agency. The most common complaint is that the State Collection Agency owed them money and, at best, made late payments. There was often a considerable delay in price information reaching the farmers, so they had to sell their products before even knowing the price. Thus, the State Collection Agency often agreed on a price at the time of sale, and later lowered the price. It was also common to hear farmers say that the agency failed to pick their crops, which were left to rot as a result.

In 2005, the state adopted measures to address these problems. First, the government issued two resolutions (187/2006 and 188/2007), whereby the collection company must pay farmers upon collecting the products. The new regulations required that payments be made either directly to the bank or through the farmer's representative in charge of financial management, and approved by the state marketing authority. In addition, the responsibility of providing price information was transferred to the boards of directors of the Provincial People's Assemblies, which had to inform producers every four months of their products' purchase price, which in turn could be negotiated by farmer representatives.

While this has led to improvements, collection problems have not been entirely resolved. For example, there is the problem of debts incurred by other agencies that farmers sell to for "social consumption," i.e., food provided to kindergartens, schools, female-headed households and the elderly.

As will be discussed below, to solve these problems, other measures were implemented at the end of the decade to resize the responsibilities of the companies involved in the marketing and distribution of agricultural food.

The Price of Discord

Based on data reported by the MFP, between 2000 and 2008 consumer prices remained high. In 2005, Resolution 53 of the Ministry of Finance and Prices (MFP) established fixed prices in order to facilitate consumer access to food. Yet during 2005, prices increased for 13 out of 21 key products. Prices have since become more decentralized, set according to provinces and municipalities as opposed to the MFP.

Another resolution issued in 2006, Resolution 243, stipulated that prices should be based on the needs of the farmer. As a result, producers are now paid a higher price for both their contracted produce as well as their surplus, which they have the option of selling to the collection agency. Triangulating data from various sources (see appendix 2), between 2003 and 2008 farmers received higher purchase prices for their products: bananas (1133%), taro (1068%), potatoes (275%) and milk (266%). This increase was made possible through increased government investment in the agricultural sector, from four billion to six billion pesos between 2005 and 2007 (ONE 2008). The result of this increased investment was a greater availability of food through the State Collection Agency, as well as greater purchasing power for farmers to access inputs such as fuel, and thus reduce crop losses.

To protect consumers from the high prices of the free market, the state negotiates prices with producers and their representatives. But there is always the risk that after negotiating a fixed price for their products one year, farmers will decide to sell their products elsewhere for a better price the next. For example, some provinces attempted to set a reduced local price for sweet potatoes in order to better serve vulnerable consumers. But the following year, it became clear that as a result, producers had not invested as much in the production of sweet potatoes, resulting in reduced availability. So the cure turned out to be worse than the ailment. When another locality recently decided to lower the price of onions, local middlemen took the opportunity to buy up the onions to sell in other provinces. Fortunately, in both cases the state intervened to renegotiate the price, rather than run the risk that farmers would stop growing sweet potatoes or that the province would run out of onions.

The Cows Grow a Conscience

"The cows grew a conscience" is how one farmer humorously explained the increased availability of fresh milk in local markets. In fact, the phenomenon is the result of a 2007 MFP resolution, which increased the price farmers received for their milk, and therefore led to increased milk production. There is now greater appreciation of the impact of prices on production and availability.

In the 1980s and 1990s, the producer price of milk stayed between 37 and 45 cents CUC per liter. In 1999, a milk-price increase was finally approved, raising the price range to 75 to 95 cents per liter. However, total milk production showed little change, since the cost of production in the state sector exceeded the purchase price. In the informal market, therefore, milk continued to be sold for three to five CUC per liter. In early 2011, the state was discussing the possibility of increasing the price of cow's milk from five to six CUC in order to keep up with the cost of production, and do away with the black market.

The case of milk is much talked about in Cuba. Beginning in September 2008, 43% of all Cuban bodegas were able to meet 100% of the demand for fresh milk. Since 2007, the price per liter of milk has been at about 2.45 CUC, increasing or decreasing according to the quality of the milk and the distance it is transported. In addition, the producer receives a bonus of two cents CUC per liter, allowing them to purchase products offered in that currency. This measure has been well received by dairy farmers. For example, farmers Orlando Ortega Delgado and his wife Maréa Josefa González report that for every liter of fresh milk delivered to the bodega, they earn from 2.48 to 2.50 CUC. They are saving up their extra 2 cents CUC to buy household appliances.

By February 2009, a number of organizations were benefiting from this new incentive, not only for the delivery of milk, but also of other products such as tubers and vegetables. The "La Miriam" UBPC, for example, has traded in its CUC credits for clothes, boots, machetes, files and other goods for its members.

This is a uniquely Cuban marketing system, rooted in a centralized model of resource distribution. The money or CUC credits received by producers for their products constitutes a bonus that gives them purchasing power in special shops managed and stocked by the state-run Agricultural Supply Company. Each municipality has its own supply company representative, to whom producers make requests for the supplies they need.

Challenges of a Fragmented Agricultural Market

Middlemen and speculators are able to take advantage of imperfections in the agricultural market for several reasons. First, since demand exceeds supply, their sales are guaranteed. Second, they often chose to sell in areas poorly served by the state distribution system. Finally, they are easily able to buy cheap and sell dear.

The intermediaries operating in the free market sell their products at the highest possible price. In an interview published in the local newspaper *Juventud Rebelde* (2008), Yunior Pupo Pérez, one of the middlemen who sells in the famous "Cuatro Caminos" market in Havana, told reporters that living as renters in the capital, "we have to fight hard." He stated he was paying a fee of 170 pesos per day to rent a space at the market, whether he made sales or not.

On the island there is much discussion about whether prices do more to favor middlemen or producers. Experts point to the absence of a consistent policy or pricing system that would minimize speculation and regulate negotiations between producers, suppliers, intermediaries, traders and consumers. On the other hand, Silvio Rodriguez from Sancti Spiritus Province indicates that speculation has diminished: "There used to be people who went to the countryside to buy cheap and sell dear on the free market. Now in order to sell, you have to submit a letter that identifies you as a producer or producer's representative. As a result, the middlemen have been

TABLE 3. Amount (pounds per product) that can be bought with 30 pesos (national currency) in different markets

Product	Youth Working Army (EJT) Market	State Agricultural Market (Mae)	Sale Points	Free Market
Garlic	1.00	2.00	2.00	5.00
Onions	4.00	7.00	7.00	10.00
Tomatoes	2.00	5.00	3.50	5.00
Sweet potatoes	0.70	1.00	1.00	3.50
Plantains	2.00	2.50	2.50	4.00
Yucca	0.70	1.00	2.00	2.50
Squash	0.70	1.00	2.00	
Cocoyum	1.00	1.50	2.00	
Beans	1.30	2.00	3.00	
Lettuce	1.50	2.00	4.00	
Cabbage	1.00	1.50	1.00	
Rice	3.50	3.50		
Carrots	0.50			
Chard	0.80			
Pork loin (1/2 lb.)	9.00			

Source: Data complied by the authors in Havana City in the Marianao, Boyeros and Vedado markets, December 2008.

1 U.S. dollar is equivalent to approximately 23 Cuban pesos

completely eliminated. There's a market on Sundays, and as a producer I can go sell there. If I don't have access to transportation, the cooperative will provide it, but if they can't, then the state will help."

Silvio's comments indicate that a blow has indeed been dealt to speculation through various policies: first, encouraging producers to increase production and product availability in the market; second, linking the buyers directly to the producers; and finally, improving the collection and distribution of quality foods through various marketing channels.

Notwithstanding these observations, speculation has not yet been eradicated, although it has fallen considerably. There was a time when the government dealt with speculation by closing the free market. It now acknowledges that the free market plays an important role in food distribution. Therefore, the government only intervenes in the free market under exceptional circumstances, as it did in the wake of Hurricanes Gustav and Ike in 2008, when it acted to contain speculation, prevent products from leaving local areas and compel farmers to sell their products to the state at reasonable prices.

The government has also taken steps to increase consumer participation in the fight against speculation. Each province now has a telephone hotline for consumers to contact a representative of the Ministry of Domestic Trade (MINCIN) to report market irregularities and violations, or to get information about agricultural markets.

Projected Changes in Agricultural Marketing

While still retaining control over 60% of domestic food distribution, the State Collection Agency is beginning to change its role in the marketing chain. It is no longer responsible for assigning prices and paying producers, thus reducing its role to accounting and consulting. Meanwhile, farmers are beginning to play a more active role.

As of 2009, a trial project called the "Operation of Production, Collection and Marketing" of agricultural products has been implemented. This plan, which for the moment covers the two Havana provinces,[13] aims to repair the linkages between production and marketing; enable greater transport efficiency; resolve financial problems in the system; and reorganize the workforce as a whole.

---

[13] Translator's note: Havana Province was divided into two provinces in January 2011: Artemisa and Mayabeque. They are referred to here as the "two Havana provinces."

TABLE 4. Agricultural marketing channels

Producers and cooperatives have a number of outlets where they can sell their products. Most contract with the state collection agency, but sell their surplus through other channels.

Market	Products
Tobacco company	Tobacco
Cocoa and coffee enterprise	Cocoa and coffee
State Collection Agency	Fruit, vegetables, meat, etc.
Town plazas	Tubers
Weekly markets	Fruit, vegetables, tubers and meat
Dairy enterprise	Milk, cheese, yogurt, butter, etc.
Beef-cattle enterprise	Beef
Pig enterprise	Pork
Small-livestock enterprise	Beef and goat meat
Specialty-fruit enterprise	Selected fruit, coconut, honey, etc.
Apiculture enterprise	Honey
Tourism enterprise	Tubers, fruit, vegetables, etc.
Agricultural free market	All surplus production, except beef
Mixed-crop enterprise	Various food crops
"Social consumption"	All surplus production, except beef
Seed enterprise	Seeds
On-farm sales	Various crops

Source: Compiled by authors based on interviews with Braulio Machín, coordinator of ANAP Sancti Spiritus, and Armando Nova, professor in the Center for the Study of the Cuban Economy (CEEC), August 2008.

Producers and cooperatives have a number of outlets where they can sell their products. Most contract with the State Collection Agency, but sell their surplus through other channels. These and other changes point to a broader process of decentralization, which is creating more streamlined institutions.

The State-Run Market Gets a New Image

In the 1990s it seemed as though the free market would eventually overtake the state-run market. In the last decade, however, the state market has not disappeared, and it has even emerged with a new image. In Pinar del Rio, for example, where numerous violations led to the closure of the free market, a state market was established in its place. In its first 14 days, the market's sales reached 700,000 pesos, and by the next month sales reached 1.2 million pesos. Investments were then made to improve the services and aesthetics of the market. For example, a fresh-fruit juice stand was built to provide juice to both workers and visitors.

In another example, the Flor de Azahar Market in Bayana (pictured below) is perhaps like no other in Cuba. With air conditioning, security cameras, and a juice and smoothie bar, Flor de Azahar borders on luxurious. In 2007, this state-run market was granted special recognition by the National Association of Urban Agriculture for the high quality and variety of its products and services.

2.5 THE RESTRUCTURING OF THE AGRO-INDUSTRIAL SUGARCANE SECTOR

The Decapitalization of the Sugarcane Sector

In the context of current transformations of the Cuban countryside, the downsizing of the sugarcane sector, which has traditionally served as the engine of the Cuban economy, deserves special attention. Since the mid-19th century and until recently, Cuba, had been the world's largest sugarcane producer and exporter. Through colonial and neocolonial eras, and even the socialist period up until the late 1980s, sugar was the country's main agricultural product, with a production capacity of eight million tons in 1985. Between 1990 and 1995, Cuba became the only country for which sugar accounted for over 90% of exports. The crop covered nearly two million hectares: 30% of the country's agricultural land.

After the collapse of the socialist bloc, the availability of agricultural inputs was restricted and sugar production fell sharply as a result. A comparison of official production figures for the periods of 1983–1984 and 2006–2007 shows a sugar production decrease of 85%. Moreover, the loss of export markets in the former socialist countries, which had previously bought Cuban sugar at favorable prices, meant a loss of $15 billion in revenue after 1990. Cuban sugar was thereafter entirely subject to international market forces (Sáenz 2007, 33).

Impacts of the Decapitalization of the Sugarcane Sector

Currently, Cuba has only 85 of the 155 mills that existed in 2002; and between 2002 and 2005 the area planted to sugarcane decreased by 52%. In recent years, as sugar exports decreased, imports increased. Since Cuba possesses insufficient refining capacity to meet the domestic demand, it must import sugar, mostly from Brazil and Colombia.

Despite the difficulties suffered by the industry, the sugarcane sector has been central to the Cuban revolution and the socialist project, not only for its role in export production, but also for its positive social impacts.

A strong network of communities emerged around the cane fields and sugar mills weaving together Agroindustrial Complexes (CAIs) or sugar towns (also known as "*bateyes*"), where social and productive life followed the rhythm of sugar production. These sites offered employment as well as important social services to the communities.

In an evaluation of Cuba's agricultural development, researchers Lucy Martín Posada and Rachel Reyes observe: "Since the soul of the towns was the sugar mill, the transformation of sugarcane culture met with some resistance. For it was not merely a productive transformation, but one that touched the lives of the people; and it was not confined to workers but also managers, young people and the Cuban people in general" (Martín and Reyes 2008).

Restructuring the Sugarcane Sector

There is broad consensus on the need to restructure the sugarcane sector. There is far less consensus, however, regarding foreign investment in the sector. Between 2002 and 2007, the government put in place a process it called the "Álvaro Reynoso Task" (TAR) aimed at downsizing the sugarcane sector. In essence, the plan consisted of a set of measures intended to increase competitiveness, reduce production costs, enhance sustainability and diversify production. The main objectives of this project were to:

- Change land-use patterns and help cane producers transition to growing a wider diversity of crops
- Increase net revenues by reducing production costs and generating greater added value
- Become self-sufficient in sugar by meeting the domestic demand of 700,000 tons
- Access foreign markets insofar as they offer prices greater than the local cost of production

Isidro Enriquez, manager of the "26 of July" sugarcane CCS in Quivicán, Havana, recounts how the process was carried out:

In 2004 there was a reorganization of land use and machinery. The soils were evaluated according to their characteristics, to determine which soils were suitable for sugarcane, livestock, mixed crops or forestry. The machinery was evaluated according to its condition, and any extra equipment was sold to MINAZ [Ministry of Sugar] for parts or scrap metal. The cooperative did continue producing sugarcane, but after 2006 it went from being purely a "sugarcane cooperative" to being a farm, and the so-called Pablo Noriega Sugar Agroindustrial Complex, which had been linked to it, was deactivated.

The restructuring was a momentous challenge, not only in economic terms, but also in socio-cultural terms. Transforming land use was also a huge challenge. As a result of the restructuring, two-thirds of the total land in sugarcane production (over 1.3 million hectares) has been converted to other crops or forest (Pérez 2000). Moreover, approximately 109,554 people associated with the sugarcane sector received retraining for other skills.

According to Tirso Sáenz, former president of the Association of Sugarcane Farmers and Technicians (ATAC), the success of the restructuring process was limited by a number of factors, such as management, allocation of resources and technology, which led to some unsatisfactory results. For example, sugarcane yields have remained low (38 tons per hectare) and industrial capacity underutilized (under 80%).

Liobel Pérez Hernández, an official in the Ministry of Sugar (MINAZ), carried out a five-year assessment of TAR, concluding that, "Although incomplete, the process of downsizing has so far had mixed results. Not all of the sites have made equal progress. (personal communication, Havana, Cuba, September 20, 2009)" Nonetheless, some cane cooperatives have been highly successful. CPA "Camilo Cienfuegos" in Bahía Honda, Pinar del Rio, for example, is today a diversified sugarcane cooperative and is among the 18 most productive sugarcane CPAs in the country.

Ethanol and Other Sugarcane Derivatives

Today, the government has high hopes for the economic potential of roughly 50 sugar by-products, including rum, paper, fertilizer and animal feed. In addition, investments are being made in ethanol production, which currently produces approximately 100 million gallons per year, of which 55% is destined for fuel. Production is expected to increase upwards of 500 million liters annually.

Technical support from Brazil and foreign investment, particularly from Venezuela, have helped the government in its push to modernize the ethanol industry, according to researcher Marianela Cordovés Herrera (Cordovés 2007), who adds that the Cuban sugarcane sector was likely to begin exporting ethanol. Venezuela will be the main recipient of Cuban ethanol, and the two governments recently signed an agreement to install 11 ethanol plants in Venezuela.

There is much international debate about ethanol. Within Cuba, some argue that ethanol is an important alternative to petroleum that Cuba should take advantage of. Others—including leader of the Cuban revolution Fidel Castro Ruz—warn of the negative socioeconomic and environmental impacts associated with the large-scale production and export of agrofuels.

2.6 FACING THE AGRICULTURAL LABOR SHORTAGE

Exodus of the Rural and Agricultural Population

Farmers frequently lament that Cuba's rural culture is being lost because there are fewer and fewer people willing to do farm work, and it is difficult to recruit workers for seasonal labor. Moreover, young people show little interest in agricultural work or in living in the countryside.

People often comment that there aren't enough incentives to work in the agricultural sector. Guantánamo farmer Hipólito Sobrado explains, "Even if you pay them well, they leave. There was one worker I was supporting: giving him clothes, good pay, even paid vacation time. And he *still* left. Nobody wants to work the land. They can make better money in the city doing almost anything else."

Observations such as these point to a serious labor shortage in the Cuban countryside, one that is supported by official statistics. Cuban experts have found that after 1967, the agricultural labor force began a continual decline until the early 1990s, caused by state restructuring of the agricultural sector and collectivization of the peasantry, a process Figueroa (2005) calls "socialist primitive accumulation." A number of pull factors have also drawn Cubans away from agriculture, such as better living conditions, employment, income, recreation and culture in the cities. The effect was magnified during the Special Period, when unemployment in the country exceeded 8% (Figueroa 2005).

A country's "agricultural density" is determined by the percentage of agricultural population per hectare of permanent cropland. The FAO (2003) reports that over the past four decades Cuba's agricultural density decreased from 1.1 (1969–1971) to 0.5 (2001–2003). Even though the rural population saw an increase of 9% (11.23 million people) between 1990 and 2007 the number of agricultural workers declined by 4% between 2006–2007 (ONE 2007). In fact, today only 11% of Cuba's rural population works in the agricultural sector, and less than 6% get their livelihood directly from agriculture (Funes-Monzote 2009). Nevertheless, agriculture continues

The need for housing is great, in both the city and countryside

One Person, One Mango Tree!

Labor scarcity is a tricky problem for the Cuban agricultural sector. Older farmers are especially worried about the possibility of passing on rural traditions to future generations.

The National Association of Small Farmers (ANAP) offers an interesting perspective. Adolfo Alvarado Esquijarosa, director of ANAP's Agro-Food Program, observes that if a farmer can't find workers, he has to look "beneath the earth" (*debajo de la tierra*), recruiting family members, neighbors and workers who might be able to provide a few hours of labor after their workday. The farmers have learned to take full advantage of any available worker and student labor.

In his opinion, the fundamental problem is not so much one of labor scarcity, but of resources. He argues that the labor force in Cuba is too elastic. He notes that it is possible to mobilize enough labor when it's required, such as in the wake of hurricanes Gustav and Ike. Braulio Machín, an ANAP member in Sancti Spiritus, also highlighted the untapped potential of mobilizing agricultural labor, stating, "If we asked each of our 29,589 members to plant one mango tree, imagine how many mangos and how many vitamins we could bring to our tables."

Even Raúl Castro Ruz has raised concerns about the need for more innovative thinking in the agricultural sector, to better organize production and empower producers to produce more food.

to employ more people than any other industry: 8.6% of the total population and 20% of the working population.

It must be noted more than 40% of the agricultural workforce is composed of researchers, service workers, managers and technical advisors not directly involved in production (Lopez 2005). This phenomenon is likely due to the historic top-down, bureaucratic approach that persists in Cuba to this day.

Return to the Countryside

In the early years of the Special Period, thousands of people began farming small plots or fostering links with farm families in order to get through the crisis. In 1993, the Cuban government formalized these new agricultural arrangements by distributing land in usufruct to more than 140,000 families. There was also a boom in urban agriculture, which emerged as an alternative solution to the crisis and became an important source of employment, engaging more than 300,000 people in urban food production.

Researcher Braulio Machín reports:

> Whether they are doctors, engineers or lawyers, the children and grandchildren of farmers [that had left the countryside] are now returning to the fields. The province of Sancti Spiritus, for example, returned to 90% of its original population as a result of new incentives in agriculture. These people never lost their rural culture. I have seen many young people who are back working on farms and in rural enterprises after getting university degrees and technical training. They still feel a strong connection with their parents' and grandparents' farms.

Beginning in the 1970s, many rural children began moving to the cities to take advantage of new education, work and cultural opportunities created by the state. Today, it is hoped that young people will be drawn by new agricultural incentives to return to rural areas.

However, the state faces a number of more subtle challenges to repopulating the countryside. For instance, in many rural communities there are few opportunities and spaces for recreation and leisure, which can result in negative social effects such as alcoholism. Hence, the government must not only improve employment and economic opportunities in rural areas, but also create opportunities for leisure and healthy recreation in order to make the countryside an attractive place to live. Machín comments on the disparity he sees between urban and rural cultural life:

> You have to have a deep love for the land to be willing to leave the city for the country. There is still no real development strategy to address this situation. I remember I used to live in a very remote area, but [Cuban singer] Benny Moré still came to perform. Now the famous orchestras don't leave Havana to travel to remote areas to entertain people, and especially young people. We need to improve [cultural conditions], as well as housing and transportation.

With respect to the labor shortage in agriculture, the government is talking about the need to improve rural incomes and link rural wages to job performance. In a recent speech, President Raúl Castro Ruz stated: "We are aware that in the midst of the extreme difficulties that we face today, wages are insufficient to satisfy people's needs, and we are not living up to the socialist principle that each should contribute according to their capacity and receive according to their work."[14]

The concept of receiving according to one's work is seen as a way to motivate people toward individual achievement, as opposed to collective work, in which it is impossible to measure individual performance. Carmelo Perez, manager of the UBPC "The Miriam" in Pinar del Rio, affirms that "providing incentives is essential. You have to hold on to the ones who are here, but how? Only by keeping them linked to their work and responsible for the final results of the work they are doing."

The Aging Rural Population

Cuba is one of the 50 countries in the world with the most rapidly aging populations. In Cuba, the life expectancy for both sexes

[14] July 17, 2007.

was approximately 78 years in 2005, while the fertility rate was 1.43 children per woman, the lowest in Latin America (ONE 2007). In addition, 77.1% of women of childbearing age use contraception, which lowers the birth rate and magnifies the extent of the aging population, both urban and rural.

Valdés Paz (2005a, 22) provides estimates that in 1987, 56% of Cuban farmers were over 60 years old and owned more than 55.4% of private lands, while those under 49 years accounted for 18.1% of producers with 18.2% of the lands. Valdés Paz also notes that aging producers face a number of challenges: 1) how to ensure the

---

The Seniors Club of Bahía Honda: Work as Exercise

In the Credit and Service Cooperatives (CCSs), the population of retirees has grown over time, but many continue working or retain their links with the cooperative. In one example, at the CPA Camilo Cienfuegos, Bahía Honda, Pinar del Rio, we had the opportunity to talk with workers Pablo Cabaña Cartete, Agapito Cajiga Herberto Cajiga, Ramón Valdés Vesoso and Lázaro Sánchez Vejerano, who were hard at work in the *organopónico*.

The four men, who average 73 years of age, are served by a social worker at the seniors club. The men work half days and use the income to pay their expenses and help their families. In addition, they are entitled to special benefits offered by the CPA to the workers. For example, mentions Luis, the club manages a special fund in case of illness.

Lázaro notes that since he has so much experience, the CPA consults him when making production and marketing decisions. Therefore, the men feel encouraged and happy to continue working. They

say they are afraid of being inactive, that if they sit back and do nothing, death will come sooner. Agapito says he wants to die *"caminando,"* in motion. Visoso says the work is like a sport. The four men are physically fit, in good spirits and have a healthy sense of humor.

replacement of this group with a new generation of farmers; 2) how to make use of idle lands and ensure greater efficiency; 3) how to expand cooperatives and the cooperative model; and 4) how to care for the elderly in rural areas.

Given the country's high life expectancy and the need to ensure a sufficient workforce, a new Social Security Act was passed in 2008 extending the retirement age from 60 to 65 for men, and 55 to 60 for women.

The Need for Agricultural Professionals

Cuba has come a long way in education and continues making progress, training professionals in all disciplines. Each province has a university and local municipal colleges. Almost every school has an agronomy and/or forestry department. Over the past 50 years, the Cuban government has made education a high priority. As a result, the country, which comprises only 2% of the population of Latin America, has 11% of the continent's scientists.

In 2007, the island had more than 31,000 technicians and nearly 7,000 agronomists, according to official data. This is despite reports of more than 3,000 agronomists and veterinarians leaving the agro-livestock sector to work in other industries. In the 1990s, a wave of agricultural professionals moved into the tourist industry, a sector that began to take over the vacuum left by the decline of the sugar economy. This exodus has been an ongoing threat to the agricultural sector, which must compete for labor with other industries that provide better working conditions and prospects for upward mobility.

Emigdio Rodríguez del Río, head of the Experimental Station for Pasture and Forage of Sancti Spiritus, comments: "We have less than fifty percent of the technicians and labor force that we need. The workers here earn about 380 pesos [monthly], but a good wage isn't enough to keep them since there are more attractive jobs available to them."

Cuban authorities have expressed concern about the "brain drain" from agricultural jobs and are working to overcome the problem. According to MINAG, the Basic Units of Cooperative Production are experiencing an "extreme" shortage of professionals, with a national average of only one agricultural professional per cooperative. Additionally, the number of university graduates per year is insufficient to meet the demand. Hence, in recent years, more support has been given for studies of the agricultural sector and additional degree programs in agriculture and veterinary science are being established at the municipal level.

The successful reincorporation of former agricultural professionals back into the sector, and of young professionals who are entering the workforce, will depend largely on the incentives that the agricultural sector can offer. In recent years, agricultural professions have increasingly become devalued vis-à-vis other career paths such as medicine and, especially, information technology. This phenomenon is seen in the strong competition for entry into

Priorities of Daily Life

As recently portrayed in a documentary by Michael Moore, Cuban health care is not only exceptional but also accessible to all Cubans. The same is true of other basic benefits, such as education, food, water, gas, electricity and public transport, goods subsidized by the state, no matter the cost.

There are many poor people in the world who dream of having these basic opportunities that have been a reality in Cuba since the 1960s. As is often said, especially when sharing a drink with friends: To health, because we already have beauty! (*¡Salud que haya, porque belleza sobra!*)

Perhaps because of the universal accessibility of medical care, health services are rarely mentioned as a priority in everyday life. For example, in an interview with the Rolando Sosa family of the "Mariana Grajales" CCS, family members listed their top household needs as bath soap, laundry detergent, clothes and shoes, in addition to more expensive goods produced abroad such as bed sheets and radios.

these disciplines, which does not exist in agriculture. Those who do enter agriculture—with the exception, perhaps, of the area of veterinary medicine—often do so as a last resort. Moreover, they often enter agro-livestock education programs as a springboard to another career track, leaving the discipline after getting high marks in their first or second year.

The shortage of trained agricultural professions has far-reaching agroecological impacts. According to Aracelis Wilson, an agricultural professional and representative of the agricultural delegation in the Havana municipality of Marianao, "to boost sustainable agriculture, and reduce the use of agrichemicals that are now entering the farms, we have to have enough professionals who are skilled in performing soil assessments, calculating the appropriate amount of fertilizers and pesticides required, and adapting crops to local conditions."

2.7 CERTIFIED ORGANIC PRODUCTION

Cuba does have a limited amount of export-oriented organic production as part of the government's strategy to boost foreign exchange earnings through exports, but also to promote sustainable agriculture. This is based on a MINAG "Organic Production Strategy" policy from 2003. These projects focus primarily on organic coffee, cacao, honey, citrus and sugar. The German company BCS Öko-Garantie, with accreditation in Europe and Asia, and the Swiss company bio.inspecta, are among the foreign certifying bodies operating in the country.

In 2001, 8,495 hectares were planted to certified organic crops, representing 0.12% of the total agricultural area. In 2007, certified organic production occupied 15,443 hectares, an increase of 82% (Chailloux 2008). However, there is a great debate about organic production. The first issue is whether the amount paid to the producer is high enough, considering the high sale price of organic products abroad. Organic producers do receive a higher price for organic products destined for export. For example, conventional coffee producers receive between eight and 21 pesos, national currency, for each tin (approx. 13 kg) of coffee. But for certified organic coffee, the payment increases to 28 pesos.

Organic farmers in other parts of the world get a much higher price than Cuban producers, whether it is for coffee, tobacco or other organic products. We also know that a cup of coffee in Europe usually costs more than one euro, whereas a producer in El Salvador, Guantánamo, is paid merely 28 pesos for a whole tin of organic coffee, and subtracted from this is 11 pesos' worth of labor time. However, this low price also must be measured against the many subsidies provided by the socialist government that are more expensive in other parts of the world, such as free universal health care, education, social security, public transport, and access to recreation, sports and culture.

The issue of a higher price for organic products compared to that for conventional products is controversial. The government's position is that a healthy diet should be available to everyone regardless of ability to pay. Unlike the elitism associated with niche organic food markets, the Cuban state perceives good food as a universal right. This is why, for example, the organic food produced by urban farmers—who are strictly prohibited from using agrochemicals by the Ministry of Agriculture—does not have special certification or a higher price. Despite these equity arguments, many people advocate labeling organics to allow consumers to make more informed choices.

It is difficult to predict if or when an internal market for organic products—accessible not only to tourists, but to all Cubans, will be established in Cuba. It will likely occur eventually, considering the rising interest in organic food consumption in Cuba, and the state's strong consumer protection laws.

Finally, there is much discussion in Cuba on the standards for organic production. The National Standardization Office, which represents the country in regional and international standard-making bodies, recently circulated a set of proposed guidelines for the production, certification, labeling and marketing of organic products for public review.

Cuba's organic production is likely to increase in coming decades. Also, given the island's socialist agricultural policy, the government has proposed offering training in participatory and community-based organic certification. This would be a big step, considering that organic certification is an issue for peasant movements throughout the world.

2.8 GENETICALLY MODIFIED FOOD AND CROPS

In Cuba, both the advocates and the critics of genetic modification (GM) in agriculture share the opinion that the public must be aware of what is happening to make informed choices about the food they consume, and to actively participate in considering the potential risks and benefits of the technology. For instance, it is widely acknowledged that non-GM crops are threatened by potential contamination from GM pollen and seeds.

Since the late 1990s, however, it has become increasingly recognized that the Cuban public is inadequately informed about GMOs (Dalmau et al. 1999; Machado Rodríguez 2005). Nevertheless, one does encounter some public concern. In a letter to the editor of the Cuban magazine *Organic Agriculture*, housewife Niurka Gómez, from a working-class neighborhood in San Miguel del Padrón, worries about "the changes they want to make to our food."

When asked about using GMOs to increase Cuban productivity, José Antonio Casimiro González, a prominent farmer in the Agroecological Movement of ANAP in Sancti Spiritus, commented, "What do you want? American soy? That soy is genetically modified! We want to grow food that is clean, healthy and ethically produced."

Biosafety Regulations and the Experimental Release of Transgenic Maize in Cuba

In Cuba the research, planting, import and export of genetically modified seeds is currently regulated by the Ministry of Science, Technology and Environment (CITMA), the Ministry of Public Health (MINSAP) and the Ministry of Agriculture (MINAG). Cuban regulations do not require labeling of GM foods, based on the principle that they are "substantially equivalent" to non-GM foods. However, Cuba has signed and ratified (September 17, 2002) the Cartagena Protocol, under the Treaty on Biological Diversity, relating to the transboundary movement of genetically modified organisms.

Since the late 1980s, Cuban scientists have been conducting research on transgenic plants resistant to pests (insects, bacteria, viruses and fungi) and pesticides. As there are no independent private research institutions in Cuba, these studies have all been carried out in the public sector. In 2008, genetic engineers at the Center for Biotechnology and Plant Engineering (CIGB) successfully produced a transgenic maize plant that produces *Bacillus thurigiensis* (Bt), allowing it to resist attacks from moths (*Spodoptera frugiperda*). The plant also contains glufosinate ammonium, the active ingredient of a group of herbicides that are marketed under the name Finale.[15] As a result, this variety of corn contains genetic information that makes it both resistant to certain pests and tolerant of a particular pesticide.

The 2008 experiments were conducted on 10-hectare plots, located in five provinces. To date no information had been disclosed about the results of these experiments.

The Debate and Warnings over GM Crops in Cuba

As elsewhere in the world, in Cuba there are diverse views and approaches on the use of GMOs in agriculture. The heart of the debate is which agricultural development is best suited to Cuba's domestic circumstances, and what is the international impact. Should the model favor agroecology, sustainable agriculture and food sovereignty, but still allow for the possibility of using GMOs? What is the impact of adopting GM crops on ecology, economics and politics.

The Center for Biotechnology and Plant Engineering (CIGB) estimates that the FR-BT1 variety of transgenic maize can yield four tons per acre without the use of chemical pesticides, thus reducing labor and economic costs, improving product quality and reducing import dependence. Proponents also claim that Cuban biotech products will not pose the same health and environmental risks as those produced by transnational companies in capitalist countries. Finally, proponents argue these products will improve Cuban food security and sovereignty as well as that of other developing countries, promising that poor countries will be able to access Cuban biotechnologies at little or no cost.

There are many others in Cuba who warn against GM crops and foods. In the book *Transgénicos: Que se gana, Que se pierde*

---

[15] Also commercially known by the names Instakil, Basta, Liberty and Rely.

Cuban Voices in Favor of GMOs

- *There is no documented scientific evidence linking globally marketed transgenic plants to health problems.*

—Marardo Pujol,
Head of the Plant Engineering Department,
Center for Biotechnology and Plant Engineering (CIGB)

- *With the necessary policies, research, marketing and bioethics, GM foods will become the path to increasing the global food supply.*

—Arline Ponce Collado and Manuel Álvarez Gil
Institute of Pharmacy and Food (IFAL), Havana University

- *It would be foolish and even suicidal not to use the tools that Cuban science has, if they are proven to be safe, in the fight against hunger.*

—Juan Carlos Borroto
Subdirector, CIGB

Cuban Voices Critical of GMOs

- *This is not just about generating opposition to GMOs, but laying the groundwork for an educated population and a meaningful debate. The development of GM products should be subjected to social oversight and control; it should break with the productivist logic of transnational corporations; and it should make a significant, qualitative difference.*

—Carlos Delgado
Department of History and Philosophy, University of Havana

- *In order to have food sovereignty we should not depend on GM crops, but rather on participatory plant-breeding techniques that involve peasants.*

—Humberto Ríos
Coordinator, Local Agricultural Innovation Program (PIAL),
Institute of Agricultural Science (INCA)

- *GM crops in Cuba will have the same effect they have had in other countries, where agriculture has no future. Agroecological models offer an endless patchwork of solutions for every problem and an alternative future that produces enough food for the Cuban people and the world.*

—Fernando Funes-Monzote
Researcher, "Indio Hatuey" Institute for Pasture and Forage

Funes-Monzote and Freyre (2009) present data and analysis by numerous experts on the risks of GMOs in Cuba and the world. The ecological, economic, political and ethical observations the authors argue against GM crops and in favor of agroecological alternatives, contrasting sharply with CIGB's positions.

Numerous articles appeared in the newspapers *Juventud Rebelde* (*JR*) and *Granma* between 1999 and 2010, reporting on the progress of CIGB research and the institution's views on the benefits and

---

Letter from Fidel Castro to a Reporter from *Juventud Rebelde* (Excerpt)

Science is proud of its achievements. Of course, many people rejoice in the ability of scientists to manipulate genes in the interest of health, but few worry about the potentially racist implications, especially when combined with imperialism and its fascist notions of a superior, globally dominant race. We must be more informed about new scientific findings in order to draw appropriate conclusions.

Every day there is news of crises in food, energy, natural resources and climate change.

Soybeans, preheated to 125 degrees Celsius, are one of the most complete sources of protein and calories among all the food products produced for human consumption, with a wide variety of uses. The GM soy, however, grown [for animal feed] to produce animal proteins and fats is unfit for direct human consumption. Legumes and grasses in general, improved [through traditional plant breeding] over centuries, are the foundation of a healthy human diet. Each different crop has specific climatic and labor requirements that influence the optimum yield attainable in each country. The production of these essential proteins and calories per hectare, and the cost (in terms of energy and CO_2 emissions) of each crop, should be in the manuals of policy makers all over the world. Having this information is perhaps just as important as knowing how to read or write. We cannot afford to be illiterate in this field.

—Fidel Castro Ruz

Taken from "Carta de Fidel a un periodista de *Juventud Rebelde*" Available from: http://www.juventudrebelde.cu/cuba/2008-06-12/carta-de-fidel-a-periodista-de-juventud-rebelde/.

prospects of transgenic crops. Little mention was made of the un-
certainties and risks of GMOs in these articles, or of the controversy
over GM crops in Cuba. The same bias often occurs in reports on
television, radio, and in magazines and scientific reports by government institutions and NGOs.

GMOs in Neighboring Countries

Among Cuba's neighbors growing GM crops, the United States
stands out as the largest producer and exporter of GM products,
with a vast area planted to these crops (soybean, corn, canola,
cotton), followed by Argentina, Canada and Brazil. CIGB reports that US corn and soybean exports to Cuba likely contain
GM grain.

In Mexico, a country very close to Cuba, there is an ongoing
struggle against GM imports and genetic contamination from experimental trials. In Bolivia, although President Evo Morales is opposed
to GM crops, in 2009 the country was the 10th largest commercial
producer of GM crops (with 0.8 million hectares) in the world, and
the eighth largest producer of GM soybeans (James 2010). Bolivia
is currently taking steps to ex-
port GM soy to the countries
of ALBA.

Ecuador's president Rafael
Correa accepts the presence of
GM products, as long as they
are regulated and controlled
in the public sector. While
Ecuador's constitutional law
and Food Sovereignty Or-
ganic Law declare that Ecuador should be "GMO-free,"
the laws contain exceptions
for GM products that serve
the national interest and that
meet health and biosafety
requirements.

Protest against transnational GM seed
companies at the World Social Forum in
Venezuela in 2006

Since 2004, Venezuelan president Hugo Chávez Frías has come out against GMOs, canceling national contracts for GM products. Chávez also rejected imports of GM products from Bolivia, vetoed Bolivia's attempts to export GM soy to ALBA countries and prohibited Venezuelan farmers from planting GM soy. The Venezuelan president has also proposed economic incentives to farmers for planting non-transgenic soybeans, but the lack of a strong regulatory framework in Venezuela weakens the government's ability to prohibit GM crops.

As political allies, Bolivia, Ecuador, Venezuela and Cuba share a certain political vision, which is partly expressed through bilateral partnerships and regional integration schemes such as ALBA, MECOSUR, Petrocaribe and the Rio Group.

Leftist social forces and peasant movements such as the Landless Workers Movement (MST) and Vía Campesina oppose the expansion of GMOs by transnational corporations because of the risk GMOs pose to rural communities, to the environment and health, and to indigenous peoples and food sovereignty.

Looking Ahead

Cuba is on the verge of losing its opportunity to be a GMO-free country by allowing GMOs at the national level. Being GMO-free seems an attainable goal given its political system, its achievements in sustainable agriculture and its island geography. Here an important paradox is emerging: GM crops are incompatible with the current policy of prioritizing sustainable agriculture.

Many warn that the acceptance of GMOs will damage the image and reputation Cuba gained for its successes in implementing the sustainable agriculture policy. To date Cuban authorities have not issued any official statements on the matter, but if the debate intensifies, they may be forced to do so. This will largely depend on the interest of the public, the mass media and policy makers to this issue.

2.9 THE PATH OF FOOD SOVEREIGNTY?

Cuba is very different from the rest of Latin America. For example, unlike Mexico, the Cuban economy has not suffered from the "dumping" of cheap imports. In Mexico, the price of corn plummeted between 1989 and 2003, causing many small farmers to sell their land and leave agriculture altogether.

Historically, the island has depended strongly on imports, and as a result of the crisis of the 1980s, food imports have increased even further. However, the recent spikes in food prices have made it difficult to import enough food to meet domestic demand. As Peter Rosset, advisor to Vía Campesina, commented in 2008, this is also an opportunity "to stay on the path of food sovereignty and sustainable agriculture."

The concept of food sovereignty also includes other objectives including the right of producers to a fair price; the right of a country to define its own agricultural and food policy; the need for genuine agrarian reform; the priority of local production for local and national consumption; the protection of peasant producers and local markets from "dumping" by developed countries; and the promotion of sustainable agriculture and access to food that is healthy, nutritious and culturally appropriate.

The current policy push, or overall agricultural policy associated with the special period, is focused on producing and diversifying roots and vegetables, the aim of which is to meet domestic demand with eight types of root crops and 16 vegetables. Increasing production of root crops is seen as a strategic way of substituting imports. However, the political concept of food sovereignty is not limited to the issue of reducing imports, nor does it necessarily require "zero imports." Rather, it argues against imports that create dependence on transnational corporations and foreign capital, thus leading to the loss of decision-making power over food and agriculture.

The country has already made enormous progress to improve income-generating opportunities in agriculture and provide better living conditions for the peasantry. Following on the pro-peasant land reforms, the state subsidizes smallholder technology "packages" that include inputs, expertise and guaranteed prices. One wonders if the sustainable rural sector might not have advanced even further if the state—in an effort to proletarianize the peasantry—had not adopted industrial agriculture during its earlier revolutionary phase. Nevertheless, the path to food sovereignty has been cleared, and the island proceeds cautiously forward.

Cuba remains on the path of food sovereignty, not only through its import substitution and agricultural development policies, but—together with ALBA and Petrocaribe—through agreements that promise to safeguard regional food sovereignty in the face of the global commodity price fluctuations. Therefore, we can speak of Cuban national food sovereignty, as well as regionally and globally.

In contemporary Cuba, the people have long been involved in making decisions on social and agricultural policies. For example, legislation such as the Social Security Law and the distribution of vacant lands were drafted after extensive consultations throughout the country. While the Cuban state recognizes and promotes the rights of peasants perhaps like no other country, it still has a long way to go.

Cuban television broadcasts educational programs that highlight the successes of sustainable agriculture

PART 3
Local Development and Sustainable Agriculture: An Experiment Worth Replicating

Cuba's agricultural policy is moving toward a model based on local, sustainable agriculture and agroecology. Part three will examine the experiences, programs and projects—governmental and nongovernmental—involved in transforming the country as a whole and increasing the potential of individuals, families, collectives, associations and institutions to produce Cuba's food. There is a perception that it is not possible to replicate the Cuban experience in capitalist countries, due to a number of macroeconomic issues such as land tenure and ownership, production, trade, distribution and consumption. We argue that the Cuban model offers many valuable lessons that might be replicated in other contexts, depending on local political and social conditions.

3.1 NATIONAL POLICIES AND LOCAL ACTION

Support for Sustainable Agriculture and Local Development

For the past two decades, sustainable agriculture has been a cornerstone of Cuban agriculture with a number of resolutions, laws and decrees relating to the environmental conservation, natural resource management and sustainable agriculture supporting it. In recent years, management of sustainable agriculture has become more decentralized, coming under the jurisdiction of the provinces, municipalities and local "People's Councils." In Cuba sustainable agriculture is more than crop management and animal husbandry, covering issues including working and living conditions; the sense of belonging and local identity of farmers; and the enrichment of personal, family and community life. Local development specialist Lucy Martín comments, "Between the articulation of macro-level policies and micro-level practices, there is room for improvisation" (Martin and Reyes 2008). Indeed, a fine web of thought and action seems to weave together local actors as they build and share knowledge and innovations.

Cubans have learned that local knowledge cannot be replaced by top-down policies. The function of macro-policies should be to accompany and support people in doing what they enjoy, and in learning, growing and succeeding. Thus, decentralization drives innovations required for local development and sustainable agriculture. This is precisely the conclusion that has been adopted at the national level. The results can be seen in the increasing authority that localities now have in determining and implementing their own agricultural programs and projects.

The Challenge of Bottom-Up Management

On the point of decentralization, Eugenio Fuster Chepe, late president of the Cuban Association of Agricultural and Forest Technicians (ACTAF), wrote: "[W]e need to decentralize without losing control, and centralize without killing [local] initiative [2006]." Combining these seemingly irreconcilable principles is the main challenge now facing the Cuban state.

Starting in the 1990s, and intensifying in recent years, there has been a lively discussion about making development more bottom-up, horizontal and participatory. The government took the task so seriously that in 2000, it passed Law 91, creating "People's Councils"[16] (Ministerio de Justicia, 2008). In 2001, it also created the Center for Local Community Development, as part of the Ministry of Science, Technology and Environment (CITMA), to be responsible for providing training and methodological support to local stakeholders. These and other measures have devolved significant power to the municipalities by decentralizing allocation of resources and also decision-making power over production, marketing and distribution. With greater local control, municipalities are better able to control the work, interests, and development strategies of local cooperatives (UBPCs, CCSs, CPAs, etc.). Decentralizing has included redistributing state functions to local bodies (municipalities and People's Councils), while still maintaining control over the economy, retaining the ability to stimulate innovation and mitigate negative circumstances.

Considering that until recently decision making was highly centralized, the participation of local actors poses a number of challenges for the country, as outlined by sociologist Mariana Ravenet in her 2005 study. The first challenge, she suggests, is eliminating top-down decision making in national policy. The second is fostering the participation of local actors in budgeting decisions and in the activities of local enterprises. Finally, there is the challenge of creating a participatory culture capable of generating local actions and managing local development.

Lucy Martín and Raquel Reyes [2008] note that agricultural development must foster integration, allowing for articulation of local experiences, while maintaining a consistent national strategy.

---

[16] Translator's note: People's Councils are representative bodies at the grassroots level and serve as the foundation of Cuba's government structure. There are roughly four to eight People's Councils per municipality, with at least three elected, paid staff members. Their offices are open to the public; they deal with local issues, and transfer information or concerns from their constituencies and neighborhood associations up to the municipal-level government assemblies.

This means combining central planning with local autonomy and forging a closer relationship between government officials and local agricultural activities.

Another major challenge is to avoid reproducing a rigid, bureaucratic centralism at the local level. State authorities have recognized the need to eliminate bureaucracy, but without affecting the state's ability to regulate the economy: a difficult balance indeed (Doimeadiós 2007).

The People as Innovators and Agents of Change

Local innovation is the cornerstone of sustainable agriculture, and empowering local innovation is the challenge of national policies. Cuba has many lessons to offer the world in this regard. Innovation in the Cuban context is conceived not as a management model or program, but rather as a generalized mind-set among the people, that they can solve their own problems.

Innovation is pervasive among the Cuban people, but it is also combined with a strong ethic of solidarity and reciprocity. During the course of our fieldwork, there were many instances in which we

Planchil devised an irrigation system using locally accessible materials like a plastic soda bottle.

hoped to see a particular piece of farmer-invented equipment, only to discover it had been given away or lent out, in solidarity.

Fortunately, Guantánamo farmer Roberto de Dios was able to share with us the homemade rice planter he invented. The machine is capable of opening the soil and dropping in seeds an equal distance apart: "I built her out of old bicycle wheels. This little machine drops seeds 15 inches apart, in rows 20 inches wide. It never fails." In most other countries, such technological innovations are patented. In Cuba, however, agricultural innovations are quickly shared and spread throughout countryside before they can even be patented.

In another example, José Antonio Casimiro González, one of the most prominent farmers in ANAP's Farmer to Farmer Agroecological Movement in Sancti Spiritus, invented a multiuse tool called a *multiarado*, for which he recently received an inventor's patent. This technology is an implement mounted to a simple frame, where you can attach tools in different positions. The tools are designed to provide multiple uses. The soil contact is minimal, giving you greater lightness and versatility, allowing you to work with a wider range of soil moistures than traditional animal traction implements. With this one tool, you can carry out all of your farming activities (Delgado 2007).

Representatives of CITMA, the National Association of Innovation and Rationalization (ANIR) and the Science and Technology Forum all confirmed that Casimiro had agreed to build *multiarados* for several farmers in the area. At the time of our interview, he was building four of them to present as gifts to the leading farmers in the province.

From these examples, it is clear that giving farmers the reins unleashes their strong desire to experiment. And experimentation always precedes innovation. We marveled at Guantánamo farmer Hippolytus Sobrado's stories: "Oh, I'm trying to plant rice between my banana trees. Looks like it's going to work. Check out this field of bananas with cilantro. They grow well in that combination."

On the other hand, it is well known that crop yields also depend on seed genetics. Since the country lacks a system for distributing productive, high-quality seeds, local innovations are critical. Thus, the state supports local, farmer-led initiatives to save and improve their own seeds.

3.2 ACCOMPANYING THE LOCAL IMPLEMENTATION OF FOOD SOVEREIGNTY

Cuba's agrarian policy is implemented through a set of programs and agricultural development projects. These are supported by government institutions like PIAL as well as nongovernmental organizations like ACTAF, ANAP and the Cuban Association for Animal Production (ACPA). Examples of such projects are given below.

Agroecological "Lighthouses"

One of the first projects of the 1990s, the Agroecological Lighthouses, sought to promote sustainable agriculture in key locations throughout the country. The project was supported by the Sustainable Agricultural Network and Extension (SANE) of the United Nations Development Programme (UNDP). A number of lighthouses were established with the additional support of ANAP (Cuba), HIVOS (Netherlands), Bread for the World (Germany) and Oxfam International (Funes et al. 2001). The Agroecological Lighthouses were established in important areas of agroecology, integrating the experience of both experts and farmers in training, research and production.

Cuba's experience with this project shows how creating a culture of dialogue among multiple stakeholders can be an opportunity for learning and a basis for scaling up agroecology (Ranaboldo and Venegas 2007).

The Farmer to Farmer Movement

The Farmer to Farmer Agroecological Movement is an ANAP program created in 1997, with the support of the German NGO Bread for the World (Machín et al. 2010). The movement's main objective is to achieve food security through sustainable means. Under the tutelage of ANAP and other supportive organizations, the movement has grown significantly since the late 1990s with farmers sharing knowledge, exchanging ideas and combining their efforts.

While the use of agrochemicals decreased between 1988 and 2007, crop production increased. For example, despite an 85%

decrease in agrochemical use in 2007, production levels reached 145% for tubers, 83% for vegetables and 351% for beans. This trend is linked to the increased use of organic matter in agriculture, as discussed in part one (ibid).

The Farmer to Farmer Movement employs a participatory methodology in which peasant "promoters" show their farms and demonstrate the techniques key to their success. Through the movement, successful examples of sustainable agriculture have multiplied. The farming demonstrations are almost always held *in situ*, or on the farm itself. For example, a farmer might demonstrate how he maintains his breeding stock of earthworms. After the demonstration, the farmers exchange ideas and make follow-up arrangements (Fundora 2008). ANAP president Orlando Lugo Fonte commented: "The development of the Agroecological Movement in Cuba is strategic; it is a question of national security. Today we have over 100,000 farmers using sustainable methods, producing organic fertilizers. We have popularized the Agroecological Movement and today these techniques are widespread and familiar to any cooperative" (Ruiz 2007).

In all its work, the Farmer to Farmer Movement is committed to a horizontal, democratic and participatory approach to development aimed at improving production, spreading agroecology techniques, and promoting the well being of families, communities and the country as a whole.

"Popular Rice"

Before the 1990s, national rice production met 60% of the internal demand, and the remaining 40% was imported. In 1989 the country produced 536,400 tons of rice; but by 1993 this figure had dropped to 176,000 tons. But then "popular rice" came to the rescue.

"Popular rice" was a spontaneous movement of people who took the initiative to plant rice in small areas, marginal lands or lowlands with water availability. The phrase refers to rice produced using local resources, with low or zero use of chemicals, and without machines. Gradually, the government intervened to support popular rice, and its production expanded.

In 1997, with very low input use, the popular rice movement succeeded in producing 140 thousand tons of rice. That same year, the Union of Rice Enterprises produced 150 thousand tons, but at a very high cost. Thanks to the popular rice program, domestic rice production was 441,600 tons in 1998. In 2001, the popular rice program produced 50% of the rice on the island, and by 2008, 75% (Funes-Monzote 2009).

The production of popular rice is based on the following principles:

- Sustainable production with minimal inputs
- Use of varieties adapted to different ecosystems
- Use of biofertilizers, biopesticides, organic matter and green manure (compost) in crop rotation systems
- Use of biodiversity
- Small-scale and medium-scale production
- Extensive use of animal traction and farmer training (Socorro, Alemán and Sánchez 2001). In 1996, the task of developing popular rice and increasing its productivity was assigned to MINAG's rice institute. At the end of the decade, MINAG issued a resolution calling for more small parcels of land to be granted in usufruct. As a result, between 1997 and 2000, between 90,000 and 100,000 new hectares of popular rice were planted. Currently, popular rice production represents approximately 70% of national production and 35% of consumption. Officials hope popular rice will be able to substitute half of the country's rice imports in coming years. To this end, 60,000 hectares of usufruct lands were distributed for rice cultivation in 2009. Measures are also being taken to improve rice purchasing, storage and distribution systems, so that the rice isn't used as pig fodder due to lack of markets, as has sometimes occurred in the past (*Granma* 2009).

The Local Agricultural Innovation Program (PIAL)

The National Institute of Agricultural Science (INCA) supports peasant seed selection through the Local Agricultural Innovation Program (PIAL). PIAL began in 2000 as the Participatory Plant Breeding

Program (PPB), established to strengthen local seed systems that had been affected by the economic crisis of the 1990s. It now serves nine of the 14 provinces, and benefits around 8,000 producers, representing 2% of all small and medium producers (Acosta 2009).

Since 2003, some of the most important local innovation projects supported by PIAL have been "agro-biodiversity fairs" and "demonstration plots," which play key roles in facilitating access to seeds, promoting genetic diversity and introducing participation. PIAL provides a wide genetic diversity of seeds to the communities involved, allowing the farmers to select the seeds that they prefer. Thus, the farmers are directly involved in selecting seeds that best meet their needs, local ecologies and socioeconomic realities.

Through the PIAL experience, it has become clear that farmers are open to experimenting and changing their production methods. According to the final report of the Participatory Plant Breeding Project (Ríos 2007), farmers have made great progress since joining the project. In one farmer's words, the project helped "open new paths."

Another important aspect of PIAL's work is supporting local innovations in soil conservation. For example, Mario "El Mocho" García in San Andres, Pinar del Rio, farms on steep slopes that sustain continuous soil loss. With PIAL's support, in 2000 he built three contour ditches to help conserve the soil. At first, García's children were not convinced of the effectiveness of ditches, arguing that they obstructed the movement of the animals. But Mario convinced them to wait and see. As a result of his commitment to soil conservation, Mario increased the production of his family's farm, and subsequently expanding it to include sugarcane, guinea grass and king grass to feed their animals. El Mocho observed, "A campesino with a small plot of land has to do what he can to make it produce."

PIAL provides important incentives to the small-farm sector. Among the program's positive impacts, PIAL participant, Vestina Mederos highlights the knowledge gained from building relationships and sharing experiences with visitors from other regions and countries. As a result of her participation in PIAL, she says she "has more love for the earth." She adds, "I wish I were twenty years younger, so I could have more energy and do even more."

Vestina, along with her husband, Sergio, and son, Sergito, is responsible for the conservation of her family's rice-seed bank; she keeps a collection of 50 varieties and supplies varieties to other farmers

The PIAL program has even changed the diet of rural families. For example, it encourages them to grow vegetables, which Cuban farmers rarely ate prior to this program. They also eat more bananas and plant their own potatoes, when roots and tubers were previously all purchased. The increase in agro-biodiversity, yields and incomes, and the reduction in external inputs are among the many positive effects of PIAL, which further encourage local innovation and sustainable agriculture (Ortiz and Schmid 2010).

PIAL coordinator and promoter Humberto Ríos notes: "Professionals make a mistake believing that we have the last word. We have to give farmers a space to farm, and offer them alternatives and choices, not just 'technological packages.'"

The National Soil Conservation and Improvement Program

In 2006, 45% of Cuban soil suffered from loss of organic matter and 70% from some other soil problem (CITMA, 2007) caused by inadequate management or weather—such as drought or heavy and prolonged rains in mountainous areas. Consequently, the government established the National Soil Conservation Program, which guides, assesses and certifies soil conservation and recovery activities.

In fact, Article 7 of the Cuban Constitution outlines the legal obligation for individuals and institutions to do everything possible to conserve the soil. It also establishes using tax dollars specifically for the purpose of funding soil conservation activities. On this basis, the National Fund for Soil Conservation was created in 2001.

The cooperatives participating in the program enter into a soil-services contract with the provincial Soils and Fertilizers Directorate. The contract details the obligations of both parties to implement soil conservation and improvement measures, with payment for each of the activities, which may include incorporating live barriers, organic matter (e.g., compost or worm castings), hedgerows, contour ditches, etc. According to Mario Riverol, head of the National Soil Conservation and Improvement Program, the program delivered between eight and nine million pesos to small farmers in 2001, its first year. By 2008 that figure had already risen to 18 million. Also, after eight years, 600,000 hectares of land—40% of all cultivated areas—are in the process of recovery. The program is expected to benefit more than three million hectares across the country, representing more than half of the country's farmland (Barreras 2009).

Given its broad coverage, the program has become increasingly important in regenerating soil damaged by agrochemical use.

National Forestry Development Fund

In addition to the Soil Conservation and Improvement Program, the National Forest Development Fund (FONADEF), created in 2000, supports farmers with funding and extension and specialized assistance in sustainable agriculture. The main objective of the fund is to promote and finance projects aimed at developing forests and protecting forest soils and resources.

In 1998, the country's forested area represented 21.03% of the national territory. By 2002, it was reported that the forested area had grown to 22.6%, an increase of 500,000 hectares (Linares Landa

2002). The National Forestry Program expects forestland to continue to grow, reaching 27% by 2015.

The payments made for reforestation services are an important incentive for farmers to plant trees on part of their land. Where the fund has been successful, it has increased forest area, with all of the environmental benefits of reforestation. Perhaps the greatest weakness of the program is that funds are often monopolized by companies, while individual farmers are rarely able to benefit (Chan 2010).

The Science and Technology Forum

The Science and Technology Forum is sponsored by the Council of State, the National Association for Innovation and Rationalization (ANIR), the National Urban Agriculture Group, MINAG and CITMA. The forum compiles data about the problems faced by each collective[17] and then convenes the workers and farmers to develop solutions. Agroecological solutions based on local knowledge and resources are promoted by the forum. The forum awards prizes to the best projects, at the grassroots level (cooperatives and companies) as well as at the municipal, provincial and national levels.

Nonetheless, interviews conducted for this research reveal that the excessive bureaucratic requirements of the program, as well as its limited human and material resources, have diminished farmers' interest in participating in the forum.

The Agricultural Extension Movement

The Agricultural Extension Movement, under the auspices of MINAG, employs a participatory approach to solving problems by introducing and disseminating agricultural innovations.

Under the Agricultural Extension System (SEA), created in 2000, MINAG aims to stimulate and support the development of technological innovations, in both the state and private sectors. The system is supported by member organizations such as MINAG and

---

[17] Translator's note: The word *collective* is used here in the broad sense, e.g., cooperatives, schools, factories, rural enterprises, etc.

the Ministry of Higher Education (MES), each of which engages in agricultural extension activities, along with producers. The system is operated in partnership with the Ministry of Science, Technology and the Environment (CITMA), which provides financial support for outreach, innovation and technology transfer and diffusion.

Organizations such as ANAP, ACTAF and ACPA participate in all of the extension projects, in addition to CITMA, the ministry in charge of science policies. Without this broad cooperation, the movement would not have had the large impact it has had throughout the country, fostering learning and knowledge sharing among farmers, researchers and policy makers.

One of the keys to the success of the Agricultural Extension Movement is its use of a diverse set of methodological tools such as oral history, song, film and photography, which express and re-create the processes. These methods also allow for the triangulation of data from various sources, such as participant observations, field notes, workshops, reports, interviews, radio and television broadcasts, publications in newspapers, brochures, newsletters, magazines and books.

3.3 URBAN, PERI-URBAN AND SUBURBAN AGRICULTURE

Growing Food in the Cities

The Urban and Peri-urban Agriculture Program began in 1990, managed by the National Urban Agriculture Group of the Institute for Research in Tropical Agriculture (INIFAT), with the participation of several other MINAG agencies.

Urban and peri-urban agriculture is defined as intensive food production within the urban and peri-urban areas. The year-round, diversified production of food in an urban environment depends on a strong understanding of the relationships between humans, nature, crops, animals, urban infrastructure and labor availability. All production in the program is based on a sustainable, closed-loop system that allows for the recycling of agricultural waste.

According to 2008 data, the Urban and Peri-urban Agriculture Program covers an area of 12,589 square kilometers, representing 14.6% of the country's total area. This figure does not represent land under production, but rather land with the potential for urban agriculture. Urban and peri-urban agriculture occupies five square meters for every Cuban citizen.

The main goal of the program is to produce as much food as possible; to increase the availability of diverse, fresh and healthy food; to produce in previously unproductive areas, using organic methods and local resources; and to market directly to consumers (Campanioni et al. 2001).

Urban and peri-urban agriculture is carried out by individuals in yards and small plots and by organized farmers in CCSs, UBPCs, state farms, *organopónicos*, intensive gardens and state self-provisioning (*autoconsumo*) areas.[18]

One of the fundamental principles of this system is decentralized production with a total of 28 sub-programs: 12 agricultural, seven livestock, and nine technical support. In addition to producing food,

---

[18] In 2006, urban and peri-urban agriculture covered between 60,000 and 70,000 cultivated hectares, depending on the time of year (Centro de Recursos para América Latina y el Caribe en Agricultura Urbana y Seguridad Alimentaria, 2000).

the livestock sub-program also provides 70% of the organic fertilizers used in the agricultural sub-programs (MINAG and Grupo Nacional de Agricultural Urbana 2007).

In addition to sustainably producing food in urban areas, the collectives and individuals involved in this process engage in a number of initiatives to protect the environment. For example, Irania Díaz, founder of the Center of Urban Waste Processing (CEPRU) in Guantánamo Province, comments:

> This used to be a horrible landfill that caused health problems, high morbidity, diarrhea and respiratory problems. There was no culture of environmental protection and the people here did not know the dangers they were exposing themselves to. I got the idea to create a different kind of landfill, and improve the environmental conditions. So I started to work here, all on my own. I used everything: bagasse [sugarcane residue], sawdust, leaves and anything available as a means of conservation. We are now marketing seeds, organic fertilizers and other products. We received an award from the United Nations, the only one ever awarded in Cuba. We also received the CNN Heroes award, which is also the only [such] prize awarded to a Cuban organization.

Irania converted a rubbish dump into an urban farm in Guantánamo City

Today Irania promotes mini CEPRU projects throughout the area and in other provinces and aspires to turn them into environmental advocacy centers. In another example, Ángel Peña, who received a master's degree in agroecology and sustainable agriculture in the 1990s, and now farms his family's land, describes his project:

> This used to be a small landfill and behind it there was a lake. Over a ten-year period, I worked on transforming it. There were three gullies, where I started improving the soil with a vegetative cover to improve the lake drainage, which was really bad. My objective was to protect the soil... I made efficient use of street water and water from a nearby stream. I'm now working on treating wastewater for use in *fertigation*.[19] We are committed to integrating and recycling everything. My mother is even recycling clothing to be used by family members or neighbors.

In addition, Ángel's agroecological farm is highly diversified, with fruit, vegetables, rice, sesame and other products for home or social consumption. He also has a dairy cow, and makes artisanal wines and juices with local fruit such as noni (*Morinda citrifolia*).

For Irania, the fundamental objective is preserving biodiversity, whereas for Ángel it is soil conservation and improvement. In both cases, the Urban and Peri-urban Agriculture Program allows each farmer to create his or her own environmental initiatives, based on his or her abilities, skills and interests. Irania and Ángel received funds from the Urban Agriculture Project, as well as other NGOs, to carry out these projects.

An Agroecological Success Story and Its Social Impacts

The Cuban urban agricultural model is based on small-scale, low external-input production, using organic matter from urban waste and by-products. It employs biological pest control, and using

---

[19] Translator's note: Fertigation is the application of fertilizers, soil amendments or other water-soluble products through an irrigation system

pesticides is legally prohibited. What's more, it is a decentralized, participatory grassroots program, but with strong government and institutional support.

Over the past 10 years the program has multiplied the total amount of fresh vegetables harvested by 1,000 percent. By the end of 2007, urban and peri-urban agriculture was producing 75% of the fresh vegetables consumed in the country, not including small family plots and backyard gardens, which are not counted (*Granma* 2009). In 2007, the Urban Agriculture Marketing Plan provided 184 grams of vegetables per person per day, representing 61.3% of the 300-gram daily requirement outlined by the FAO (Puente 2006).

Urban agricultural production has grown in recent years. In 2008, it produced more than one million tons of fresh fruit and vegetables. (Nodals 2008). This has been achieved without using agrochemicals. Moreover, urban agricultural production provides vegetables to day-care centers, single-parent homes, nursing homes, elementary schools and hospitals, among other institutions.

In addition to its achievements in production, urban agriculture also provides jobs and income. Between 2005 and 2009, urban agriculture employed more than 384,000 people, 21% of whom were women, 10% retired people and 20% youth. The basic salary is approximately 200 pesos a month, in addition to receiving 50% or more of the profits obtained from product sales (Herrera 2009).

The Urban and Peri-urban Agriculture Program covers a radius of 10 kilometers from the center of each of the 14 provincial capitals, five kilometers from the center of the municipal capitals, and two kilometers from the center of towns of more than 10,000 inhabitants.

Beginning in 2009, the Suburban Agricultural Program was implemented in 17 suburban municipalities. According to Raúl Castro Ruz, in a speech to the National Assembly of People's Power (August 1, 2009), suburban lands should be developed to provide work for local residents and reduce fuel expenditures. He commented:

> We have to forget about this notion of tractors and fuel. Even if we had enough of them, our goal should be to do the work

with oxen, as it is done on small farms with excellent results by a growing number of farmers. I have visited places where they've converted their land into veritable gardens that make use of every square inch of land.

Also managed by the National Urban Agriculture Group, the Suburban Agriculture Program aims to apply the same principles as the Urban and Peri-urban Agriculture Program. The program was tested with a pilot project in the province of Camaguey and in some Havana municipalities. In addition to producing food sustainably using agroecological methods, the Suburban Agriculture Program works to improve marketing and distribution systems. The program is being developed 10 kilometers outside cities and towns and two kilometers outside villages with 1,000 inhabitants.

3.4 ENSURING GENDER EQUITY IN AGRICULTURE

Gender-Equity Work in Cuba

Since 1959, Cuba has focused on the problem of gender inequity. Following the revolution, the Federation of Cuban Women (FMC) was created to coordinate and promote women's emancipation, participation, welfare and empowerment at the national level. Cuban women have benefited from a number of social policies, implemented in the wake of the revolution, including access to education, health, employment and social security. Before 1959 women represented 12% of the employed workforce and by the end of the 1990s, they represented 42%.

The crisis of the Special Period had little effect on women in the workplace, given that at that time they comprised a small percentage of the blue-collar workforce (Caram 2005). However, sociological research conducted in the late 1990s found that women accounted for 72% of the professional workforce including education, and 67% of the health sector. ONE (2007) reported that in 2006 women accounted for 66% of all technicians and professionals.

In the 1960s and 1970s, women made up 40% of higher education students; increasing in the early 1980s, to 57%; and by the 1990s 70% of the student population.

In terms of women's access to leadership positions, progress has been slower, given the sexism and strong gender biases in the culture.

The female labor force is increasingly important

In 1980, for every 100 employed men, 10.7 were in leadership positions, while 5.4 women occupied leadership positions for every 100 women. In 2002, for every 100 men employed, 12 occupied leadership positions, while only 6.7 out of every 100 women were leaders (Echevarría 2003; ONE 2007).

Still, a tremendous amount of work has been done to promote gender equity, such as promoting the participation of women on equal terms; improving access to and quality of social services for women; increasing awareness through gender-sensitivity training; and generating statistics and indicators about gender. Such projects are carried out by a variety of government ministries and nongovernmental organizations, such as ACTAF, ACPA and ANAP.

Achievements and Obstacles to Overcome

In 2009, ONE reported that rural women accounted for 47% of the rural population and for a little more than 11% of the Cuban population as a whole (Dixie 2009).

The countryside is generally characterized by much more conservative gender relations, especially with regard to women's roles being limited to the domestic sphere (Martínez and Leiva Hoyo 2006). Indeed, from 1997 to 2001, women's employment in farming was around 18% (Martín and Reyes 2008). This may be attributed to the high degree of difficulty of farm work and difficult working conditions.

Ynorbis Lezcaille Brooks, a member of ACPA in Guantánamo, comments on women's evaluation of the organization's gender strategy: "They almost always asked for improved working conditions: better bathrooms, eating places, hygiene and all those things you know are important to women." Female workers at the UBPC "La Miriam" observed that "work in the fields is very hard" and they would change occupations if they could find something better. They said they worked in the fields out of necessity, "because there isn't anything else" (Chan 2008).

However, women are becoming an important part of the agricultural labor force, either in their homes, workplaces or in rural communities. Their presence is especially strong in agricultural development programs such as the Urban and Peri-urban Agriculture

Program, which has 67,576 women, representing nearly 20% of the workforce. In 2007, in a televised roundtable discussion, Dr. Maria del Carmen Perez from the Ministry of Agriculture said the women's participation in the Urban Agriculture Program has the potential to grow, but it must be actively promoted.

The most successful UBPCs we visited during the course of this research paid special attention to the participation of women. For example, at the UBPC "La Miriam" (mentioned above) in Pinar del Rio, 22% of the members and 40% of the board of directors are women (Chan 2008).

Cuba has made advances toward gemder equity in the agricultural sector. A recent study on social mobility in Cuba states, "Rural women are the group that has benefited the most in education and employment, showing the effectiveness of strategies targeting the most disadvantaged groups" (Martín and Reyes 2008).

Edith, who runs a flower *organopónico* in Sancti Spiritus, remarked that she wants to hire more women because she thinks they work better than men, and take better care of flowers. However, there are limitations that prevent women from taking these jobs. For example, there are not enough day-care centers for young children, or for older children during school breaks. As a result, women are often forced to quit their jobs or bring children to their workplace. In addition, workplace conditions are often poor, without access to water or bathrooms. The work schedule also tends to favor men over women, who require greater flexibility so they can meet family obligations.

The work of women tends to be hidden in the domestic sphere. This is especially the case for rural women, who contribute to the economic, social and cultural production of the household and are vital pillars of stability in rural life. This invisibility of their work is due to the fact that they often don't work directly in the fields, and few possess land titles: only 11% of landowners are women, according to ANAP figures. ANAP Coordinator Braulio Machín comments, "Behind the numbers of partners and cooperative members it is not easy to see the women, whose workday often extends beyond twelve hours a day... We need to make agriculture more flexible and lighten the demands on labor time and work schedules."

Of course, in many rural families, women are engaged in raising animals and growing fruit, vegetables, herbs and medicinal plants in backyard and kitchen gardens for family consumption. In one interview, when asked, "What does Juana María do?" the husband replied, "She never worked until we started to participate in this seed-diversification project." The wife immediately protested, "How is it that I never worked? I worked every day in and around the house!" It's not that the husband did not appreciate the work of his wife. He was simply reflecting a deep-seated stereotype, that only paid work is important.

Women currently can be cooperative members, whether or not they own land. However, in order to increase women's self-esteem, employment opportunities and participation in decision making, there is a need for both subjective and objective changes. Braulio Machín comments:

> When women participate as full members in the cooperatives, they have more opportunities to attend meetings and access leadership positions… Often, when couples are members of a cooperative, the man is the one who attends the meetings, while the woman stays at home… If she stays isolated at home, she loses the chance to expand her social relationships beyond the family. But at least if she is a member, she has greater possibility of realizing her social potential, and she is more likely to participate in decisions… As a full member, she can participate in the cooperative assembly; she has a voice; she can vote and be elected. That is a social opportunity.

> Of course, it's about more than participation. Women now receive all the associated benefits [of cooperative membership], such as having the opportunity to go on an exchange trip to another part of the country or abroad… But I think you have to keep in mind that we have not achieved equity in domestic activities, nor have we achieved the best possible conditions for women working in the fields. If a woman has to work in the home in addition to working in other fields, then she's going to have a double burden. Far from being emancipated, she'll be overwhelmed.

Strategies and Experiences of Gender Work in the Rural Cooperative Sector

ANAP stands out as one of the organizations working to implement programs and projects with a specific focus on gender. Its gender strategy includes the following objectives:

- Achieving greater involvement of women in the CPAs and CCSs, and strengthening women's participation in various levels of management and decision making
- Increasing gender awareness throughout ANAP's leadership structure, through training and advice from the Federation of Cuban Women (FMC)

The strategy is based on gender committees composed of members of ANAP, FMC and other agencies and organizations from each region, including cooperatives. For instance, ANAP has implemented a pilot project for increasing gender awareness among men, women and families belonging to cooperatives.

In Cuba, as in other parts of the world where farming is the main source of employment, women have difficulty accessing jobs. In other words, insufficient diversity of employment is a constraint to women's access to employment. Indeed, ANAP's gender work is geared specifically to changing this situation that is associated with agriculture and the rural sector.

A cooperative director of ANAP's Gender Program commented:

I won't say it was easy to combine the role of wife, homemaker, mother and worker. Sometimes even my hair hurts. But my husband and the other cooperative members always supported me. Imagine me, a peasant girl from Caujerí Valley. I couldn't imagine that anyone would listen to me, much less elect me to the central committee. At that time I was pregnant with twins. I didn't even have any clothes. How I cried! They took me to go buy clothes and then I gave birth two months later. That's when I understood that they take women into account, because we have a lot to offer, too.

Juan Carlos Loyola Flobat, coordinator of the pilot project for the implementation of ANAP's gender strategy, highlights the importance of ensuring not only quantity, but quality, in women's participation. To this end, the project works with women in cooperatives, but also those that work in the home, offering training to help them achieve their goals. An important part of the work is increasing the visibility of women and highlighting their ability and potential to be leaders. The project uses popular education tools including participatory workshops, in which both men and women participate.

ANAP's gender strategy has shown modest achievements, mostly in women's access to senior positions, with a small increase in women's access to cooperative membership and land titles. Between 2006 and 2008, the number of women in management positions grew by 7.1%, the number of women cooperative members grew by 0.8%, and the number of women landowners grew by 0.2%. However, it is expected that implementing the new land-distribution policy will increase the number of women with usufruct titles and cooperative membership.

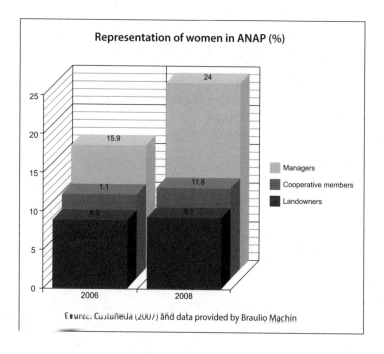

Source: Castañeda (2007) and data provided by Braulio Machín

3.5 THE REPLICABILITY OF THE CUBAN EXPERIENCE

While Cuba's agricultural policies are grounded in a unique social, political and organizational history, that experience offers a number of principles perfectly adaptable to countries facing the adverse consequences of neoliberal globalization. For example, despite recent setbacks, the Cuban state has not abandoned its political will to ensure social services such as health care, nutrition, education and social security. These services benefit all Cubans—in the countryside and in the city; black, white and mulatto; women and men; young and old. Even the most remote parts of the countryside they have access to electricity, water, schools and medical services.

The Cuban example illustrates that food is a national security issue, in which the international goals of reducing hunger can only be realized through public policies that place domestic food consumption as a top, and nonnegotiable, priority.

The Cuban government's agricultural policy demonstrates how the decentralization of power, production and markets can be carried out without causing social exclusion and marginalization; indeed, that local and national development can be in harmony. Cuba demonstrates

Representatives from the Democratic People's Republic of Korea interested in Cuba's agricultural development participate in a sustainable agriculture event.

the revolutionary potential of the small-farmers' lifestyle and mode of production, and the benefits of promoting cooperative democracy and sustainable agricultural development. In fact, many countries in the region, such as Venezuela, Bolivia and Nicaragua, have made similar commitments not only to economic development and trade, but also to social values such as health, education and food security.

For three decades, Cuba has shared its experience and knowledge of agroecology with other countries. For example, ANAP offers agroecological training to foreign students and farmers at its "Niceto Pérez" National Farmer Training School. Cuba also provides agro-ecological training and support to countries including Brazil, Bolivia, Ecuador, Venezuela and Mexico. The island also hosts renowned conferences, attracting the participation of citizens from around the world who are interested in Cuba's agroecological experience.

Cuba also serves as a benchmark for countries like North Korea, which also faces US sanctions. Although the two countries have very different climate and ecology, the agroecological principles Cuba has applied could be replicated in other contexts. It is important to note that local development programs do not require massive amounts of state resources. If a small country like Cuba can achieve international recognition for its sustainable agriculture, countries with far greater resources could obtain substantial results.

In Cuba, the large-scale shift toward sustainable agriculture is the result of the will and innovations of small farmers, with strong support from the Cuban state. In light of the issues raised in this report, it should be clear that the potential for replicating the Cuban experience in sustainable agriculture lies mainly in the political will of the state, in the motivation the people and, perhaps most importantly, in the relationship between the two.

Children put on a skit in which they play members of a cooperative

Conclusions

Some say this is a new nation, a land newly awakened.
I say it is a fruit, a seed, a light, and all of our dreams…
José Cruz, "Winter"

"Produce more, have more!" So read government billboards placed throughout Havana in early 2009. The billboards were followed by others, with slogans relating to import substitution, conserving energy, economic efficiency and labor discipline. Appeals reflecting the high priority now given to food production are also heard on the news, television and radio programs as well as in workplaces and schools.

But where is Cuban agricultural policy headed? The widespread enthusiasm among producers in both the cities and countryside; the agricultural production trends of the last 10 years; and the transformation of Cuban agricultural policies; all point to a great potential for producing more food to replace the island's imports, and producing it ever more sustainably.

Cuba has a number of important accomplishments in production, marketing and consumption:

- It has shown that a country can increase domestic food production using low-external-input agriculture, by capitalizing on local resources and local conditions.
- It has distributed idle land to people with the resources, knowledge and skills to sustainably produce food on them.
- It has diversifyed the country's species and crops, thus diversifying the diets of Cuban citizens.

- It has made advances in decentralizing agriculture and reducing the state's ownership of land.
- It has strengthened and supported cooperatives that showed a high capacity for organization, administration, production and distribution.
- It has increased state support for farmers in the form of subsidies, social recognition and higher prices for their products.
- It has stimulated local production and marketing, thus improving local food security.
- It has raised awareness among farmers and built consensus around the need to transition to organic agriculture based on principles of agroecology, dialogue and cooperation.

These achievements indicate that the country has taken significant steps toward achieving food security and sovereignty. The main agents of change have been farmers, policy makers, professionals and technicians, who have contributed their knowledge and worked together to meet these goals.

Cuban farmers take pride in producing healthy food for their people. They are eager to demonstrate how, for example, they can produce enough food for up to 15 people on just one hectare of land. They also recognize that despite the enormous efforts they make on a daily basis, Cuba has yet to exploit its full potential.

Indeed, Cuban agriculture remains an unfinished puzzle that continues to face a host of challenges, such as:

- Improving access to basic resources for agricultural work, in both rural and urban areas
- Creating a more efficient system of transportation for the timely collection and distribution of food and agricultural products
- Creating effective market mechanisms that meet the needs of both producers and consumers
- Fostering participatory, horizontal cooperation among local communities and the organizations and agencies that provide management support, technical assistance and financing

- Where agrochemicals are used, promoting their limited use to avoid dependence on imports and vulnerability to external shocks
- Creating better conditions and incentives for the production and marketing of certified organic food, for both domestic consumption and export
- Weighing the risks that transgenic seeds and other Green Revolution approaches pose to the country's achievements in organic agriculture, sustainability and climate change
- Increasing opportunities for women to access jobs and leadership positions in rural areas

How is this small Caribbean country facing global climate change, neoliberal globalization and the international food and financial crisis?

First, it is important to note that despite these momentous challenges Cuba has held on to its important social achievements. At the Sixth Congress of the Cuban Communist Party in April 2011, measures were approved to enhance trade relations, and autonomous monetary management and decentralization. But this "updated" socialist model continues to provide free health care and education, with predominant public ownership and an orientation toward sustainable agriculture. Indeed, the many social benefits and opportunities enjoyed by Cuban citizens have allowed the country to withstand the global crises that have undermined the quality of life in most countries.

Nonetheless, the global food crisis has turned food security into a top, nonnegotiable priority toward which the entire country's efforts, both rural and urban, are to be directed. In the midst of this crisis, Cuba has offered its solidarity and humanitarian aid to other parts of the world in the form of health care, education, sustainable agricultural development, science and technology, and disaster relief, as well as denouncing the injustices committed against countries of the Global South.

Other countries are also reaching out to Cuba. Through new humanitarian relationships and regional integration schemes, the island is now better positioned to share its experiences.

Professors Nilda and Carlos teach integrated pest management in Laos, part of a project of Focus on the Global South and Oxfam Solidarity Belgium

Columbian Eduard Pinzón completed an internship in sustainable agriculture in Cuba; the Cuban government offered him a scholarship to study at the Agrarian University of Havana

In the eyes of many outsiders, Cuba's experience in agricultural, economic and social development represents a complex puzzle. This book has sought to shed light on Cuba's agricultural system by addressing the following questions:

What makes Cuba so unique in terms of its experience with sustainable agriculture, local development, food security and food sovereignty?

First, the state has maintained its political commitment to ensuring and sustaining its social achievements.

Second, private and state management of Cuban markets operate without interference from transnational corporations or conditional, neoliberal policies imposed by the World Bank, IMF and WTO.

Third, despite the global food, fuel and financial crisis, Cuba has maintained its protections for producers and consumers, and continues to guarantee basic access to food for all its people.

As such, Cuba provides a unique example of a socioeconomic system designed for the purpose of ensuring food security and sovereignty (Wright 2009).

Is the Cuban experience replicable in other Latin American countries and in the rest of the world?

The Cuban experience in agricultural and social development offers principles that are perfectly adaptable to countries facing difficult circumstances imposed by neoliberal globalization. Local development programs are an integral part of any holistic program for sustainable rural development. If a small country such as Cuba can achieve international recognition for sustainable agricultural development, countries with far greater resources at their disposal could achieve similar, or better, results. In this light, the replicability of Cuba's successes lies primarily in the willingness of states and of their people.

Cuba continues to be one of the few examples in which the sustainable agriculture movement receives strong state support, in addition to popular support among farmers and the general population.

And that is the key: political will.

REFERENCES

1. Acosta, Dalia. 2009. "Agricultura-Cuba: Innovación en manos campesinas." Agencia de Noticias Inter Press Service (IPS). (Accessed December 5, 2011.) http://ipsnoticias.net/print. asp?idnews=87100.

2. Aguiloche Añé, Lia. 2006. "Contribución a los estudios de pobreza en Cuba." Una caracterización de la Capital. (Accessed July 13, 2012.) http://focal.ca/pdf/cuba_Ane%20Aguiloche_reforma%20 economica%20poblacion%20Habana_July%202005_Mexico.pdf.

3. ANAP (National Association of Small Farmers). 2006. *Informe del decrecimiento de asociados en las CPA durante el año 2005 y el primer trimestre de 2006.*

4. ANPP (Asamblea Nacional del Poder Popular). 1991. *El programa alimentario.* Havana: Editorial José Martí.

5. Arruda Sampaio, Plinio. 2005. "La Reforma Agraria en América Latina: una revolución frustrada." *Reformas agrarias y luchas por la tierra en América Latina.* Observatorio Social de América Latina (OSAL), year 6, January–April.

6. BBC Mundo. 2007. "Cuba, tras la exportación de etanol." March 16. (Accessed December 1, 2011.) http://news.bbc.co.uk/hi/spanish/business/newsid_6458000/6458147.stm.

7. BBC. 2009. Richard Black. "'Many hurricanes' in modern times." UK: August 13. (Accessed August 14, 2012.) http://news.bbc. co.uk/2/hi/8197191.stm.

8. Borrego, Mary Luz. 2009. "Cuba. desarrolla un maíz transgénico. La primera plantación, experimental, en el valle de Caonao." *Juventud Rebelde*, March 2.

9. Borroto, Carlos G. 2010. Letter to Narciso Aguilera Marín in relation to his article "Alerta ecologista contra la promoción de maíz transgénico en Cuba." *Rebelión*, May 23. (Accessed July 13, 2012.) http://www.rebelion.org/noticia.php?id=106382.

10. Burchardt, Hans-Jürgen. 2000. "La última reforma agraria del siglo: cambio o estancamiento." In *La última reforma agraria del siglo: La agricultura cubana, entre el cambio y el estancamiento* edited by Hans-Jürgen Burchardt, 169–94. Caracas, Venezuela: Nueva Sociedad.

11. Campanioni, Nelson, Egidio Páez, Yanet Ojeda and Catherine Murphy. 2001. "La agricultura urbana." In *Transformando el campo cubano. Avances de la agricultura sostenible*, Edited by Fernando Funes, Luis García, Bourque Martín, Nilda Pérez and Peter Rosset. Havana: Asociación de Técnicos Agrícolas y Forestales (ACTAF). Havana.

12. Caram León, Tania. 2005. "Mujer y poder en Cuba." In *La Gobernabilidad en América Latina: balance reciente y tendencias a futuro*. Universidad de La Habana: Facultad Latinoamericano de Ciencias Sociales (FLACSO). (Accessed July 17, 2012.) http://bibliotecavirtual.clacso.org.ar/ar/libros/cuba/flacso/caram.pdf.

13. Castañeda Pérez, Isabel, 2007. Aproximación al Estudio de la equidad de género en la ANAP: Premisas Para Un Diagnóstico. (Accessed August 14, 2012.) http://www.flacsoandes.org/dspace/bitstream/10469/1169/1/Aproximaci%C3%B3n%20al%20estudio%20de%20la%20equidad%20de%20g%C3%A9nero...%20Isabel%20Casta%C3%B1eda.pdf.

14. Castro, Fidel. 1985. "Discurso de clausura del VII Periodo Ordinario de la Asamblea Nacional del Poder Popular, celebrada el 28 de diciembre de 1984." *Granma*, January 4.

15. Cavero, Teresa, and Carlos Galián. 2008. "Double-Edged Prices. Lessons from the food price crisis: 10 actions developing countries should take." Oxfam International: Oxfam Briefing Paper 121. (Accessed July 17, 2012) http://www.oxfam.org/en/policy/bp121-double-edged-prices.

16. Centro de Recursos para América Latina and el Caribe en Agricultura Urbana y Seguridad Alimentaria. 2008. "Agricultura urbana en Cuba, ¿un modelo exportable de alivio a la crisis alimentaria?" *Boletín de Agricultura Urbana*, no. 9–10, April–September. (Accessed November 28, 2011.) http://www.ipes.org/au/Boletin/boletin9/au_cuba.html.

17. CEPEC (Centro de Promoción del Comercio Exterior y la Inversión Extranjera de Cuba). 2008. "Las exportacines de servicios en Cuba." (Accessed November 28, 2011.) http://www.cepec.cu/exportaservicioscuba.php.

18. Chailloux, Marisa. 2008. "Comercialización de productos agro ecológicos y orgánicos en Cuba." Asociación Nacional de Técnicos Agrícolas y Forestales (ACTAF). Resúmenes del III Encuentro Nacional de Agricultura Orgánica. Las Villas, April.

19. Chan, Mayling. 2008. "La Miriam. Voces y expectativas de una UBPC exitosa." *Revista Agricultura Orgánica*, year 14, no. 3: 2–6.

20. ———. 2010. "La política incentivos para producción agrícola sostenible en Cuba." PhD thesis. Agrarian University of Havana.

21. Chiotti Alaimo, María Inés and Braulio Machín-Sosa. 2008. Sistematización de experiencias. El Valle de Caujerí y el Valle de los Ingenios. Havana: Edited for Oxfam by Asociación Nacional de Agricultores Pequeños (ANAP).

22. CIGB (Centro de Investigaciones en Ingeniería Genética y Biotecnología). 2009. Maíz FR-Bt1: variedad sintética de genotipo amplio, resistente a la palomilla del maíz y tolerante al herbicida glufosinato de amonio. PowerPoint presentation. May 9.

23. CITMA (Ministry of Science, Technology and Environment). 2007. Estrategia Ambiental Nacional (2007-2010). Havana: Editorial CITMA.

24. Communist Party of Cuba. 1975. *Tesis y Resoluciones Del Primer Congreso Del Partido Comunista de Cuba*. Havana: Editora Política.

25. Cordovés Herrera, Marianela. 2007. "Cuba, tras la exportación de etanol." BBC Mundo. March. (Accessed July 16, 2012.) http://news.bbc.co.uk/hi/spanish/business/newsid_6458000/6458147.stm.

26. *Cuba Encuentro*. 2008. "El déficit comercial sigue siendo alto, pese al aumento de las exportaciones." Agencias. April 24. (Accessed July 13, 2012.) http://www.cubaencuentro.com/cuba/noticias/el-deficit-comercial-sigue-siendo-alto-pese-al-aumento-de-las-exportaciones-80799.

27. *Cuba hoy*. 2009 "En marcha estrategia para sustituir importación de arroz en Cuba hoy." November 21. (Accessed December 1, 2011.)

http://cubahoy.over-blog.es/article—en-marcha-estrategia-para-sustituir-importacion-de-arroz-en-cuba-hoy—39754509.html.

28. Dalmau, Enrique, María Victoria Valdés Rodda, Margarita McPherson Sayú and Jorge Mario García. 1999. "Organismos modificados genéticamente: educación, información y percepción pública. Biotecnología Aplicada." *Journal of the Sociedad Iberolatinoamericana de Biotecnología Aplicada a la Salud* 16: 57–61.

29. Delgado Díaz, Ricardo. 2007. "José Antonio Casimiro González: ¿Productor o creador?" *Revista Agricultura Orgánica*, no. 2: 8.

30. Dixie, Edith. 2009. "Cuba: Las que miran a la tierra." *SEMLAC: Servicio de Noticias de la Mujer de Latinoamérica y el Caribe* (Accessed November 28, 2011.) http://www.redsemlac.net/noticias/2009/090706de.htm.

31. Doimeadiós, Yaima. 2007. "Un modelo de crecimiento económico para Cuba: Un análisis desde la productividad de los factores." PhD thesis. Department of Economics, University of Havana.

32. Echevarría, Leon Dayma. 2003. "Mujer, empleo y dirección en Cuba: algo más que estadísticas." In *Sociedad Cubana hoy*, edited by Alain Basail Rodríguez (coordinator). Havana: Editorial Social Sciences.

33. EFE. 2011. "Cuba will spend 25% more on food imports due to rising prices." (Accessed July 17, 2012.) http://www.cubadebate.cu/noticias/2011/04/15/cuba-gastara-25-mas-en-importacion-de-alimentos-por-alza-internacional-de-precios/.

34. FAO (Food and Agriculture Organization of the United Nations). 2003. *Estadísticas de Densidad Agrícola-Cuba*. Rome: FAO.

35. ———. 2004. The State of Food and Agriculture 2003-2004. Agricultural Biotechnology: Meeting the needs of the poor? Rome: FAO. (Accessed July 19, 2012.) http://www.fao.org/docrep/006/Y5160E/Y5160E00.htm.

36. ———. 2007. *Perfil nutricional de Cuba*. (Accessed July 17, 2012.) ftp://ftp.fao.org/es/esn/nutrition/ncp/cubmap.pdf.

37. ———. 2008. *World Food Commodity Prices*. Rome: FAO-OECD.

38. ———. 2009. "Los precios de los alimentos permanecen muy altos en muchos países." July 16. (Accessed November 28, 2011.) http://www.fao.org/news/story/es/item/28803/icode/.

39. Fernández, Jaime. 2005. "Los huracanes no dependen del cambio climático." *Tribuna Complutense*, October 11.

40. Fernández Novo, Mario, and Fernando Funes. 2010. "Saludos y pa´lante, Fuster." *Revista Agricultura Orgánica*, no. 3: 17. (Accessed July 17, 2012.) http://www.actaf.co.cu/revistas/revista_ao_95-2010/Rev%202010-3/AO2010-3.html.

41. Figueroa Albelo, Víctor. 1995. "La reforma económica en el sector agrario." In *El sector mixto en la reforma cubana*. Havana: Editorial Félix Varela.

42. ———. 2005. "Los campesinos en el proyecto social cubano." *Revista Temas*, no. 44. Ministry of Culture, Havana.

43. Fundora Mayor, Zoila. 2008. "El mensaje de Campesino a Campesino: un intercambio sobre técnicas claves en Bahía Honda, Pinar del Río." *Revista Agricultura Orgánica*, no. 2: 33. ACTAF. (Accessed July 17, 2012.) http://www.actaf.co.cu/revistas/revista_ao_95-2010/Rev%202008-2/RA2008-Mensaje.pdf.

44. Funes, Fernando, Luis García, Martín Bourque, Nilda Pérez and Peter Rosset, eds. 2001. *Transformando el campo cubano. Transformando el campo cubano. Avances de la agricultura sostenible*. Havana: Asociación de Técnicos Agrícolas y Forestales (ACTAF).

45. Funes-Monzote, Fernando R. 2008. "Farming like we're here to stay: The mixed farming alternative for Cuba." PhD thesis. Wageningen University, The Netherlands.

46. ———. 2009. *Agricultura con futuro. La alternativa agroecológica para Cuba*. Matanzas: Editorial Indio Hatuey.

47. Funes-Monzote, Fernando R., and Eduardo Francisco Freyre Roach. 2009. *Transgénicos: Que se gana, Que se pierde*. Félix Varela Center of Havana. Havana: Editorial Acuario.

48. Fuster Chepe, Eugenio. 2006. "Diseño de la agricultura urbana cubana." *Revista Agricultura Orgánica*. ACTAF No.2. (Accessed July 17, 2012.) http://www.actaf.co.cu/revistas/revista_ao_95-2010/Rev%202006-2/05-Diseno.pdf.

49. García Álvarez, Anicia. 2007. "Sustitución de importaciones de alimentos en Cuba: Necesidad vs. posibilidad." (Accessed July 17, 2012.) http://www.nodo50.org/cubasigloXXI/economia/galvarez3_310003.pdf.

50. García Álvarez, Anicia, and Betsy Anaya Cruz. 2009. "Economía y población en Cuba: Actualidad y Perspectiva." *Boletín Cuatrimestral del Centro de Estudios de la Economía Cubana, no.2*, April. (Accessed July 17, 2012.) http://www.ceec.uh.cu/sites/default/files/Econom%C3%ADa%20y%20 Poblaci%C3%B3n.%20Anicia%20Garc%C3%ADa%20y%20 Betsy%20Anaya.pdf.

51. González, Ana Margarita. 2009. "Entrega de tierras (II): Con premura, pero sin chapucerías." *Trabajadores*, July 13:12.

52. Grogg, Patricia. 2009. "Maíz transgénico llega al surco cubano." *Tierramérica*, April 16. (Accessed November 28, 2011.) http:// www.tierramerica.info/nota.php?lang=esp&idnews=3247&co lt=416.

53. ———. 2009. "Transgénicos: No basta la buena fe." Interview with Eduardo Francisco Freyre Roach. Inter Press Service (IPS)– Corresponsalía Cuba, year 22, no. 7, April. (Accessed July 17, 2012.) http://cubaalamano.net/sitio/client/issue.php?id=1667.

54. Guerrero Borrego, Natividad. 2009. "Género y diversidad: Desigualdad, prejuicios y orientación sexual en Cuba." *Temas*, no. 14, April–July: 27.

55. Gurian-Scherman, Doug. 2009. *Failure to yield: Evaluating the performance of genetically engineered crops*. Cambridge, MA: Union of Concerned Scientists.

56. Herrera Sorzano, Angelina. 2009. "Impacto de la agricultura urbana Cubana," año 5 número 9. Revista Electrónica Novedades en Poblacíon. ISSN: 1817- 4078. (Accessed July 17, 2012.) http://www.cedem.uh.cu/sites/default/files/Impacto%20de%20 la%20agricultura%20urbana%20en%20Cuba.pdf.

57. James, Clive. 2010. Global Status of Commercialized Biotech/ GM Crops: 2010. Brief for the International Service for the Acquisition of Agri-biotech Applications (ISAAA). (Accessed November 28, 2011.) http://www.isaaa.org/resources/publications/ briefs/42/default.asp.

58. Kintto, Lucas. 2004. "Ecuador: ¿Un futuro de transgénicos?" SERVINDI-Servicios de Comunicación Intercultural, July 25. (Accessed November 28, 2011.) http://www.servindi.org/actu- alidad/4383.

59. Levins Richard. 2005. "How Cuba is going ecological." *Capitalism Nature Socialism,* 1548-3290, 16: 3, 7–25.

60. Linares Landa, Elías. 2002. "Ley forestal de Cuba. Incentivos y alcance. Taller regional sobre sistemas agroforestales y su potencial en América Latina." (Accessed July 17, 2012.) http://www.cedaf.org.do/eventos/forestal/Legislacion/Incentivos/Cuba.pdf.

61. López, Teodoro. 2005. "Organización y estructura del sistema de extensión agraria (SEA) en Cuba." (Accessed July 17, 2012.) www.cipav.org.co/RevCubana/fullart/1201/120102.doc.

62. Machado Rodríguez, José Manuel. 2005. Plantas y alimentos transgénicos: percepciones sociales. *Temas,* no. 44, September–December, 65–73.

63. Machín Sosa, Braulio, Adilén María Roque Jaime, Ávila Lozano, Dana Rocío Ávila Lozano and Peter Michael Rosset. 2010. *Revolución agroecológica: El Movimiento de Campesino a Campesino de la ANAP de Cuba.* Havana: ANAP.

64. Martín, Lucy, and Raquel Reyes. 2008. *El alma del municipio era el ingenio. Cinco años de acompañamiento del desarrollo agropecuario en Las Tunas.* Havana: Edited for ACTAF, ACPA, ANAP, and Oxfam.

65. Martín, Marianela, and León Haydée. 2009. "Experimentarán nueva fórmula para el acopio y comercialización de productos agrícolas." *Juventud Rebelde,* June. (Accessed July 17, 2012.) http://www.juventudrebelde.cu/cuba/2009-06-07/experimentaran-nueva-formula-para-el-acopio-y-comercializacion-de-productos-agricolas/ 2009.

66. Martínez Massip, Annia, and Lázaro Leiva Hoyo. 2006. "Reflexiones en torno al contexto social de la ama de casa rural." *Sexología y Sociedad*, year 12, December.

67. ME (Ministerio de Economía). 2008. "Situación de las Solicitudes de Tierra al Amparo del Decreto Ley 259." October 20.

68. MINAG (Ministerio de la Agricultura) and Grupo Nacional de Agricultura Urbana. 2007. "Lineamiento para Subprogramas de la Agricultura Urbana para 2008–2010 y Sistema Evaluativo." Havana: ACTAF.

69. MINJUS (Ministerio de Justicia). 2008. Gaceta Oficial de la República de Cuba. Havana, no. 24. August 29. (Accessed August 14, 2012.) http://www.gacetaoficial.cu/.

70. Nodals, Adolfo Rodríguez (Director, National Urban Agriculture Group). 2008. Presentation at the National Convergence of Organic Agriculture.

71. Nova González, Armando. 2006. *La agricultura en Cuba (1959–2005). Evolución y trayectoria.* Havana: Editorial Ciencias Sociales.

72. ———. 2008. "La producción de leche y la sustitución de alimentos importados." *Boletín Cuatrimestral del CEEC,* April. Havana.

73. ———. 2009. "La Producción Agrícola y Pecuaria 2008." *Boletín Cuatrimestral del CEEC,* April. Havana.

74. ———. 2010. "Agricultura." Miradas de las Economía Cubana. Havana: Editorial Caminos.

75. Nutrinet.org. 2008. "Situación nutricional en Cuba." (Accessed December 2, 2011.) http://cuba.nutrinet.org/cuba/situacion-nutricional.

76. Ojeda, Ricardo Bruno. 2010. "La deforestación: un fenómeno que amenaza la vida del hombre." *Periodico Granma.* Havana, March 22. (Accessed July 19. 2012.) http://www.granma.cu/espanol/2010/marzo/lun22/La-deforestacion.html.

77. ONE (Oficina Nacional de Estadística de Cuba). 2007. *Cuba: Indicadores seleccionados.* Havana.

78. ———. 2008. *Cuba: Indicadores seleccionados.* Havana.

79. Ortiz, R., Angarica Lydia and Misteli Marguerite Schmid. 2010. "Diseño y evaluación participativa de efectos directos (cambio de actitud) en proyectos de innovación agropecuaria local," *Cultivos Tropicales* 31, no. 4: 12–19.

80. Oxfam International. 2008. "Double-Edged Prices: Lessons from the food price crisis: 10 actions developing countries should take." October 15. (Accessed August 14, 2012.) http://www.oxfam.org/en/policy/bp121-double-edged-prices.

81. Pagés, Raisa, and René Castaño. 2006. "Acopio tiene ahora la palabra: No podemos ser parásitos de los productores." *Granma,* February 17.

82. Peña Castellanos, Lázaro. 2006. "Globalización y desarrollo local: Una visión desde la actualidad de la academia Cuba." In *Desarrollo local en Cuba*, edited by Ada Guzón Camporredondo, 17–45. Havana: Editorial Academia.

83. Pérez Villanueva, Everleny. 2000. "La reestructuración de la economía cubana. El proceso en la agricultura." In *La última reforma del siglo: La agricultura cubana, entre el cambio y el estancamiento*, edited by Hans-Jürgen Burchardt. Caracas, Venezuela: Nueva Sociedad.

84. ———. 2009. "Apuntes sobre las importaciones cubanas desde Estados Unidos." *Boletín Cuatrimestral de CEEC*, April.

85. Pfeiffer, Dale Allen. 2005. "Cuba—una esperanza." *Aprendiendo de la experiencia: Las crisis agrícolas en Corea del Norte y Cuba (Parte 2)*. May 9. (Accessed December 2, 2011.) http://www.rebelion.org/noticia.php?id=14858.

86. Prensa Latin. 2009. "Cuba, alta producción de agricultura urbana." May 21. (Accessed July 17, 2012.) http://www.2000agro.com.mx/agriculturaprotegida/cuba-alta-produccion-de-agricultura-urbana/.

87. Puente Nápoles, José. 2006. "La agricultura urbana asume el abastecimiento de hortalizas a círculos infantiles, escuelas y hospitals." *Revista Agricultura Orgánica*, year 12, no. 2. ACTAF.

88. Ranaboldo, Claudia, and Carlos Venegas. 2007. "Escalonando la agroecología. Procesos y aprendizajes de cuatro experiencias en Chile, Cuba, Honduras y Perú." Mexico: Plaza y Valdés/IDRC. (Accessed December 2, 2011.) http://www.idrc.ca/en/ev-114950-201-1-DO_TOPIC.html.

89. Ravenet Ramírez, Mariana. 2005. "Los estudios comunitarios desde una perspectiva especial." (Accessed July 17, 2012.) http://www.uh.cu/centros/cesbh/Archivos/bvirtual/Mariana1.pdf.

90. Ribeiro, Silvia. 2008. "¿Quiere bajar la producción? ¡Use transgénicos!" *Fortín Mapocho*. (Accessed December 2, 2011.) http://www.fortinmapocho.com/detalle.asp?iPro=1740&iType=134.

91. Ríos, Labrada Humberto. 2007. *¿Y ahora qué? Seis años de trabajo de Fitomejoramiento Participativo en Cuba.* Unpublished report.

92. Rodríguez Cruz, Francisco. 2007. "Favorable situación ambiental en Cuba" *Periodico Trabajadores*, December 22. Órgano Central de Trabajadores de Cuba (CTC).

93. Rodríguez Nodals, Adolfo. 2006. "Síntesis histórica del movimiento de agricultura urbana de Cuba." *Revista Agricultura Orgánica*, year 12, no. 2. ACTAF.

94. Rodríguez, José Luis. 2007. "Presentación del Informe sobre los resultados económicos del 2007, y los lineamientos del plan económico y social para el 2008." *El Economista de Cuba*, February. Havana: La Asociación Nacional de Economistas y Contadores de Cuba (ANEC).

95. Pérez Rojas, Niurka, and Dayma Echevarría León. 2006. "Las Unidades Básicas de Producción Cooperativa cubanas (1993–2003)." Analysis for a debate. In *La construcción de la democracia en el campo latinoamericano* by Hubert C. de Grammont. March. Buenos Aires: Consejo Latinoamericano de Ciencias Sociales (CLACSO).

96. Rosset, Peter. 2007. "Mirando hacia el futuro: La Reforma Agraria y la Soberanía Alimentaria." In *AREAS, Revista Internacional de Ciencias Sociales*, no. 26. (Accessed July 25, 2012.) http://revistas.um.es/areas/article/view/118571.

97. Rosset, Peter, and Martín Bourque. 2001. "Lecciones de la experiencia cubana." In *Transformando el campo cubano. Avances de la agricultura sostenible*. Havana: ACTAF.

98. Ruiz, Antonio. 2007. "Valora la ANAP la estrategia agroecológica." *Revista Agricultura Orgánica*, no. 2:3. Havana: ACTAF.

99. Sáenz, Tirso C. 2007. "La agroindustria de la caña de azúcar en cuba del siglo XXI." In *XXX Convención Nacional de la Asociación de Técnicos Azucareros de México*. September. Veracruz.

100. Sánchez Egozcue, Jorge Mario, and Juan Triana Cordoví. 2008. "Un panorama actual de la economía cubana, las transformaciones en curso y sus retos perspectives." *Documento de Trabajo*, no. 31.

101. Sinclair, Minor, and Martha Thompson. 2001. "Cuba, Going Against the Grain: Agricultural Crisis and Transformation." Oxfam America Report, June. (Accessed July 25, 2012.) http://www.oxfamamerica.org/publications/cuba-going-against-the-grain/. PDF.

102. Socorro, Miguel, Luis Alemán and Salvador Sánchez. 2001. "El cultivo popular del arroz." In *Transformando el campo cubano: Avances de la agricultura sostenible*. Havana: ACTAF.

103. Soitu.es. 2008. "Científicos cubanos trabajan para plantar transgénicos de forma masiva en Cuba." February 12. (Accessed December 2, 2011.) http://www.soitu.es/soitu/2008/12/02/info/1228250385_901088.html.

104. Spanish.china.org.cn. 2009. "Cuba reduce las importaciones de alimentos de Estados Unidos." (Accessed December 2, 2011.) http://spanish.china.org.cn/international/txt/2009-11/09/content_18852093.htm.

105. UNESCO (United Nations Educational, Scientific and Cultural Organization). 1999. "La ciencia para el siglo XXI: Un nuevo compromiso." World Conference on Science. June 26. Budapest, Hungary.

106. US–Cuba Trade and Economic Council, Inc. 2008. *Economic eye on Cuba©*.

107. Valdés Paz, Juan. 2005a. "Los campesinos en el proyecto social cubano." *Revista Temas*, no. 44, October–December.

108. ———. 2005b. *Procesos Agrarios en Cuba*. Havana: Editorial Félix Varela.

109. ———. 2006. "Cuba: Hacia una tercera reforma agraria." Centro Peruano de Estudios Sociales (CEPES). (Accessed July 17, 2012.) http://www.cepes.org.pe/debate/debate25/06_Articulo.pdf.

110. ———. 2009. "Los desafíos del acopio agropecuario." ProgresoSemanal.com, May 21–27. (Accessed December 2, 2011.) http://progreso-semanal.com/index.php?option=com_content&task=view&id=834&Itemid=5.

111. Varela Pérez, Juan. 2009. "Si acopio no funciona." *Granma*, January 6:16.

112. ———. 2011. "Hasta el fondo en las tierras ociosas." *Granma*, year 15, no. 25, January 25. (Accessed December 2, 2011.) http://www.granma.cubaweb.cu/2011/01/25/nacional/artic01.html.

113. Wright, Julia. 2009. *Sustainable Agriculture and Food Security in an Era of Oil Scarcity. Lessons from Cuba*. London: Earthscan.

APPENDICES

APPENDIX 1:

Percentage of agricultural production per type of farm January–May 2008 Unit of measurement: metric tons					
Product	Total	State Sector	UBPCs	CPAs	CCS and individual farmers
Tubers (taro, sweet potato, yucca)	543	107.4 20%	104.8 19%	63.5 11%	267.3 50%
Vegetables	845.2	228.9 27%	40.3 5%	34.4 4%	541.6 64%
Rice	36.8	10.5 28%	12 33%	1.0 3%	21.0 36%
Corn	36.5	3.2 9%	1.9 5%	1.6 4%	29.8 82%
Beans	32.1	2.0 6%	1.6 5%	2.5 8%	26.0 81%
Fruit	118.3	16.7 14%	8.8 8%	5.2 4%	87.6 74%
Data Source: Agricultural sector indicators, ONE January–May 2008					

APPENDIX 2:

Price paid to producers at the State Collection Agency, in pesos per 100 kg 1 USD: Approximately 23 pesos				
Product	**1993**	**2003/2004**	**2006**	**2008** **(First half)**
Paddy rice	27	-	-	330
Black beans	123	836	990	990
Corn (feed)	-	-	264	374
Sweet potatoes	17	17	40	132
Taro	27	35	220	374
Plantains	-	33	330	374
Yucca	18	18	44	110
Potatoes	-	20	29	55
Avocados	-	-	88	176
Tomatoes	-	42	-	330
Papayas	16	-	88	176
Coffee (by the can)	-	31	31	46
Milk (by the liter)		0.9	0.9	2.4
Pork	2 por 1 kg.	-	48 por 1 kg.	37*
Beef	-	7 per kg	7 per kg	14 per kg

* Cuban pesos for each kg less than 75 kg. And 24 for each kg more than 75 kg.

Source: Compiled by the authors based on data provided by Zoraida Pedroso Pedroso, specialist of the Ministry of Finance and Prices, in October 2008; ANAP; ONE; the MINAG delegation of Sancti Spiritus; and Rolando Sosa, president of the CCS "Mariana Grajales," Sancti Spiritus, August 2008.

ACRONYMS

ACPA   Cuban Association of Animal Production

ACTAF   Cuban Association of Agricultural and Forest Technicians

ALBA   Bolivarian Alliance for the Americas

ANAP   National Association of Small Farmers

ANEC   National Association of Economists and Accountants of Cuba

ANIR   National Association for Innovation and Rationalization

CCS/F   (Strengthened) Credit and Services Cooperative

CEEC   Center for the Study of the Cuban Economy

CEPES   Peruvian Center for Social Studies

CEPRU   Center of Urban Waste Processing

CIGB   Center for Biotechnology and Genetic Engineering

CITMA   Ministry of Science, Technology and Environment

CPA   Cooperative Agricultural Production

CUC   Cuban Convertible Peso

EJT   Youth Labor Army

FAO   Food and Agriculture Organization of the United Nations

FMC   Federation of Cuban Women

PPP   Participatory Plant Breeding

FTA	Free Trade Agreement
FTAA	Free Trade Area of the Americas
IMF	International Monetary Fund
INCA	National Institute of Agricultural Science
INIFAT	Institute for Research in Tropical Agriculture
HDI	Human Development Index
MAE	State Agricultural Market
MERCOSUR	Southern Common Market
ME	Ministry of Economy
MES	Ministry of Higher Education
MFP	Ministry of Finance and Prices
MINAG	Ministry of Agriculture
MINAZ	Ministry of Sugar
MINCEX	Ministry of Foreign Commerce
MINCIN	Ministry of Domestic Trade
ONE	National Statistics Office
NGO	Nongovernmental Organization
PIAL	Program for Local Agricultural Innovation
TAR	"Álvaro Reynoso Task"
UBPC	Basic Unit of Cooperative Production
UN	United Nations
UNAH	Agrarian University of Havana
UNDP	United Nations Development Program
WB	World Bank
WTO	World Trade Organization

UNFINISHED PUZZLE

CUBA 2011

ABOUT FOOD FIRST

Food First, also known as the Institute for Food and Development Policy, is a nonprofit research and education-for-action center dedicated to investigating and exposing the root causes of hunger in a world of plenty. Our 36 years of research have revealed that hunger is caused by poverty and injustice—not scarcity. Resources and decision-making are in the hands of a privileged few, depriving the majority of land, profits, living-wage jobs, and healthy food.

Founded in 1975 by Frances Moore Lappé, author of the best-selling *Diet for a Small Planet*, and food policy analyst Dr. Joseph Collins, Food First has published over 60 books, including the seminal *Food First: Beyond the Myth of Scarcity*. Hailed by the New York Times as "one of the most established food think tanks in the country," Food First's groundbreaking work continues to shape local, national and international policies and debates about hunger and development.

Through books, reports, videos, courses, projects, media appearances, speaking engagements and conferences Food First amplifies the voices and directly supports the work of the social movements forging equitable, sustainable solutions to hunger—rural and urban—around the globe.

More from Food First Books

Food Movements Unite!

Strategies to Transform Our Food System
Edited by Eric Holt-Giménez

This book brings the words, insights and visions of the remarkable farmers, workers, and consumers from rural and urban communities around the globe as they address the critical question: "How can we unite to transform the global food system?"

Paperback, $24.99, also available as an e-Book and in the Italian language

Food Sovereignty

Reconnecting Food, Nature and Community

Edited by Annette Desmarais, Nettie Wiebe and Hannah Wittman

This book argues that food sovereignty is the means to achieving a system that will provide for the food needs of all people while respecting the principles of environmental sustainability, local empowerment and agrarian citizenship.

Paperback, $24.95, also available as an e-Book

Food Rebellions

Crisis and the Hunger for Justice

Eric Holt-Giménez and Raj Patel with Annie Shattuck

This book gives a detailed historical analysis of the events that led to the global food crisis and documents the grassroots initiatives of social movements working to forge food sovereignty around the world.

Paperback, $19.95

Beyond the Fence

A Journey to the Roots of the Migration Crisis

Dori Stone

This book examines how US/Mexico policy affects families, farmers, and businesses on both sides of the border, exposing irretrievable losses, but also hopeful advances. Companion DVD, Caminos: The Immigrant's Trail, with study guide.

Paperback, $16.95

Agrofuels in the Americas

Edited by Rick Jonasse

This book takes a critical look at the recent expansion of the agrofuels industry in the US and Latin America and its effects on hunger, labor rights, trade and the environment.

Paperback, $18.95

Alternatives to the Peace Corps

A Guide to Global Volunteer Opportunities, Twelfth Edition

Edited by Caitlin Hachmyer

This easy-to-use guidebook is the original resource for finding community-based, grassroots volunteer work—the kind of work that changes the world, one person at a time.

Paperback, $11.95

Campesino a Campesino

Voices from Latin America's Farmer to Farmer Movement for Sustainable Agriculture

Eric Holt-Giménez

The voices and stories of dozens of farmers are captured in this first written history of the farmer-to-farmer movement, which describes the social, political, economic and environmental circumstances that shape it.

Paperback, $19.95

Promised Land

Competing Visions of Agrarian Reform

Edited by Peter Rosset, Raj Patel and Michael Courville

Agrarian reform is back at the center of the national and rural development debate. The essays in this volume critically analyze a wide range of competing visions of land reform.

Paperback, $21,95

Sustainable Agriculture and Resistance

Transforming Food Production in Cuba

Edited by Fernando Funes, Luis García, Martin Bourque, Nilda Pérez, and Peter Rosset

Unable to import food or farm chemicals and machines in the wake of the Soviet bloc's collapse and the tightening US embargo, Cuba turned toward sustainable agriculture, organic farming, urban gardens, and other techniques to secure its food supply. This book gives details of that remarkable achievement.

Paperback, $18.95

The Future in the Balance

Essays on Globalization and Resistance

Walden Bello. Edited with a preface by Anuradha Mittal

A collection of essays by global south activist and scholar Walden Bello on the myths of development as prescribed by the World Trade Organization and other institutions, and the possibility of another world based on fairness and justice.

Paperback, $13.95

Views from the South

The Effects of Globalization and the WTO on Third World Countries

Edited by Sarah Anderson

Foreword by Jerry Mander, Afterword by Anuradha Mittal

This rare collection of essays by activists and scholars from the global south describes, in pointed detail, the effects of the WTO and other Bretton Woods institutions.

Paperback, $12.95

Basta!

Land and the Zapatista Rebellion in Chiapas, Third Edition

George A. Collier with Elizabeth Lowery-Quaratiello

Foreword by Peter Rosset

The classic on the Zapatistas in its third edition, including a preface by Rodolfo Stavenhagen.

Paperback, $16.95

America Needs Human Rights

Edited by Anuradha Mittal and Peter Rosset

This anthology includes writings on understanding human rights, poverty and welfare reform in America.

Paperback, $13.95

Education for Action

Undergraduate and Graduate Programs that Focus on Social Change, Fourth Edition

Edited by Joan Powell

An authoritative and easy-to-use guidebook that provides information on progressive programs in a wide variety of fields.

Paperback, $12.95

We encourage you to buy Food First Books from your local independent bookseller; if they don't have them in stock, they can usually order them for you fast. To find an independent bookseller in your area, got to www.booksense.com.

Food First books are also available through major online booksellers and through the Food First website, www.foodfirst.org. You can also order directly from our distributor, Perseus Distribution, at (800) 343-4499. If you have trouble locating a Food First title, write, call, or e-mail us:

Food First
398 60th Street
Oakland, CA 94618-1212 USA
Tel: (510) 654-4400
Fax: (510) 654-4551
E-mail: foodfirst@foodfirst.org
Web: www.foodfirst.org

If you are a bookseller or other reseller, contact our distributor, Perseus Distribution, at (800) 343-4499, to order.

Films from Food First

The Greening of Cuba

Jaime Kibben

A profiling of Cuban farmers and scientists working to reinvent a sustainable agriculture based on ecological principles and local knowledge.

DVD (In Spanish with English subtitles), $35.00

America Needs Human Rights

A film told in the voices of welfare mothers, homeless men and women, low-wage workers, seniors, veterans, and health care workers.

DVD, $19.95

Caminos

The Immigrant's Trail

Juan Carlos Zaldivar

Stories of Mexican farmers who were driven off their land, forced to leave their families and risk their lives to seek work in the US

DVD and Study Guide, $20.00

How to Become a Member or Intern of Food First

Join Food First

Private contributions and membership gifts fund the core of Food First/Institute for Food and Development Policy's work. Each member strengthens Food First's efforts to change a hungry world. We invite you to join Food First. As a member you will receive a 20 percent discount on all Food First books. You will also receive our quarterly publications, Food First News and Views and Food First Backgrounders, providing information for action on current food and hunger issues in the United States and around the world. If you want to subscribe to our internet newsletter, People Putting Food First, send us an e-mail at foodfirst@foodfirst.org. All contributions are tax-deductible.

You are also invited to give a gift membership to others interested in the fight to end hunger.

Become an Intern for Food First

There are opportunities for interns in research, advocacy, campaigning, publishing, media and publicity at Food First. Our interns come from around the world. They are a vital part of the organization and make the work possible.

To make a donation, become a member, or apply to intern just write, call or visit us online at

Food First
398 60th Street
Oakland, CA 94618-1212 USA
Tel (510) 654-4400
Fax (510) 654-4551
E-mail: foodfirst@foodfirst.org
Website: www.foodfirst.org